ॐ यो ध्व ल ह्र ह्रां ह्रीं ह्रू ह्रैं ह्रौं ह्रः ॐ यो ध्व ल ह्र ह्रां
श लोक नाथस दानाद दान वत्सर लैं व क्षा हृष्टिक राय विश्वं ल्यालनाय लोक नाथस दानाद
कायि महानूर श्री लाय यं म न्त्र व दद ध्यैं क कवि श्यामि ब ल म हृद्धिद्र्य यिम हानूर श्री लाय यं म न्त्र
कस्त स्थि क यो क्त र्गुण कय न जा नन्दि ज्ञ ज्ञा ह्रिष्टंध्व बाव न का कौं श्री व दिश कस्त स्थि क यो क्त र्गु
मान किमं क किर्ज्जि विश्चा स्नि मद्वि च्छा मया वत्स स्व मंज्ञ मज्गुरा मज्झं मन्त्र मान किमं क किर्ज्जि व
व क रु ४ य च्छा यद्का मनु श्याइं का क ल य ल य मं त्रि लो क्या चा धि ॐ व क रु ४ य च्छा
श्री मझ्म नायाधी   द व द व महा   ब कं दिक किं चा री गी श्री मझ्म नायाधी
रु ह्रां नाथा य व रु ण क य ब गा दा म व क नकौं व द र्हा मा रं रु ह्रां नाथा य व रु ण
वा व क्यं दि नु व स्य   मि   च क्ष्या क्षि नाथ य म वा व क्यं दि नु व स्य
रु ग व रु क ठ ४ गृ ष्टि ला   य ना   व ना   य दि क क्ष्या क्षुं रु ग व रु क ठ ४ गृ ष्टि
का म वा ज क रे ह्रै मा य   ल क्षी व का म वा ज क रे ह्रै मा य
मा त्रं ण ड वा म व न व र्जि कं   वा ख्यं व क्ष्या मि स र्व ग श्या मा त्रं ण ड वा म व न
ॐ मा य क्षः   यो ध्व ल ह्र ह्रां ह्रीं ह्रू ह्रैं ह्रौं ह्रः ॐ यो ध्व ल ह्र ह्रां
श लोक नाथस   दानाद   व क्षा   हृष्टिक   ल्यालनाय लोक नाथस दानाद
कायि महानूर श्री लाय यं म न्त्र व   द ध्यैं क कवि श्यामि ब ल म हृद्धिद्र्य यिम हानूर श्री लाय य
कस्त स्थि क यो क्त र्गुण कय न जा न   न   ह्रिष्टंध्व बाव न का कौं श्री व दिश कस्त स्थि क यो क्त र्गु
मान किमं क किर्ज्जि विश्चा स्नि मद्वि च्छा मया वत्स स्व मंज्ञ मज्गुरा मज्झं मन्त्र मान किमं क किर्ज्जि व
व क रु ४ य च्छा यद्का मनु श्याइं का क ल य ल य मं त्रि लो क्या चा धि ॐ व क रु ४ य च्छा
श्री मझ्म नायाधी ष्ठ ड वा द व द व महा द व स र्व लो क दिक किं चा री गी श्री मझ्म नायाधी
रु ह्रां नाथा य व रु ण क य ४ ब गा दा म व क थन कौं व द र्हा मा रं रु ह्रां नाथा य व रु ण
वा व क्यं दि नु व स्य मि ना व का ना क्ष्या क्षि नाथ य म वा व क्यं दि नु व स्य
रु ग व रु क ठ ४ गृ ष्टि ना र्ग य व ज्ञ क म ह्र दि क क्ष्या क्षुं रु ग व रु क ठ ४ गृ ष्टि
का म वा ज क रे ह्रै मा य ल क्ष्मी ध्व का म वा ज क रे ह्रै मा य
मा त्रं ण ड वा म व न व र्जि कं ध्या नं व क्ष्या मि स र्व ग श्या मा त्रं ण ड वा म व न

Anthony Francisco concept art.

MARVEL STUDIOS
THE INFINITY SAGA

THE ART OF
MARVEL STUDIOS
DOCTOR STRANGE

WRITTEN BY
JACOB JOHNSTON

FOREWORD BY
SCOTT DERICKSON

AFTERWORD BY
ALEXANDRA BYRNE

BOOK DESIGN BY
ADAM DEL RE

DUSTJACKET ART BY
RYAN MEINERDING

DOCTOR STRANGE CREATED BY
STAN LEE & STEVE DITKO

TITAN BOOKS

FOR MARVEL PUBLISHING
JEFF YOUNGQUIST, Editor
SARAH SINGER, Editor, Special Projects
JEREMY WEST, Manager, Licensed Publishing
SVEN LARSEN, VP, Licensed Publishing
DAVID GABRIEL, SVP Print, Sales & Marketing
C.B. CEBULSKI, Editor in Chief

FOR MARVEL STUDIOS 2016
KEVIN FEIGE, President
LOUIS D'ESPOSITO, Co-President
VICTORIA ALONSO, Executive Vice President, Visual Effects
STEPHEN BROUSSARD, Senior Vice President, Production & Development
WILL CORONA PILGRIM, Creative Director, Research & Development
KEVIN WRIGHT, Production & Development Manager
RYAN POTTER, VP Business Affairs
ERIKA DENTON, Clearances Director
RANDY McGOWAN, VP Technical Operations
AXEL SCHARF, Production Asset Manager
DAVID GRANT, Vice President, Physical Production
ALEXIS AUDITORE, Manager, Physical Assets

MARVEL STUDIOS: THE INFINITY SAGA - DOCTOR STRANGE: THE ART OF THE MOVIE

ISBN: 9781803368443

First edition: May 2025

10 9 8 7 6 5 4 3 2 1

Published by Titan Books
A division of Titan Publishing Group Ltd
144 Southwark St, London SE1 0UP

www.titanbooks.com

© 2025 MARVEL

No similarity between any of the names, characters, persons, and/or institutions in this book with those of any living or dead person or institution is intended, and any such similarity that may exist is purely coincidental.

Did you enjoy this book? We love to hear from our readers. Please e-mail us at: readerfeedback@titanemail.com or write to Reader Feedback at the above address.

To receive advance information, news, competitions, and exclusive offers online, please sign up for the Titan newsletter on our website: www.titanbooks.com

No part of this publication may be reproduced, stored in a retrieval system, or transmitted, in any form or by any means without the prior written permission of the publisher, nor be otherwise circulated in any form of binding or cover other than that in which it is published and without a similar condition being imposed on the subsequent purchaser.

A CIP catalogue record for this title is available from the British Library.

Printed in China

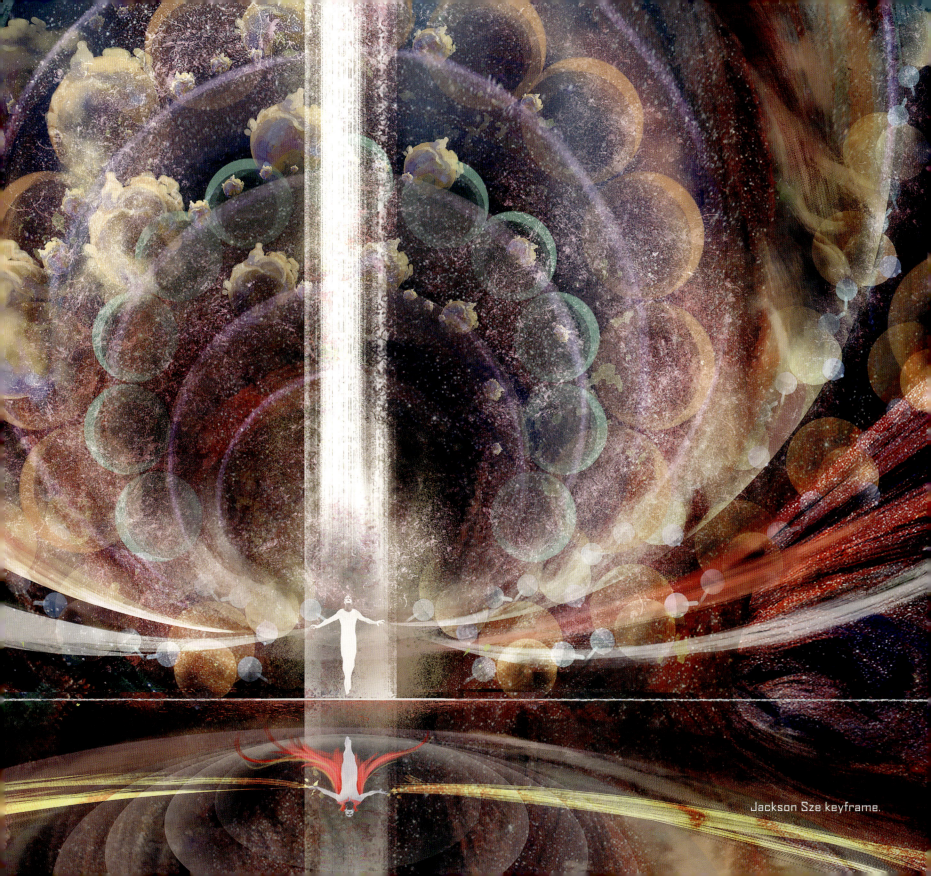
Jackson Sze keyframe.

Ryan Lang concept art.

CONTENTS

8 FOREWORD
BY SCOTT DERRICKSON

10 INTRODUCTION
THE IMPOSSIBILITIES ARE ENDLESS...

14 CHAPTER ONE
TRAGEDY AND REBIRTH

72 CHAPTER TWO
"EVER SEE THAT IN A GIFT SHOP?"

136 CHAPTER THREE
MASTERING THE MYSTIC ARTS

164 CHAPTER FOUR
WHAT IS UNSEEN IS ETERNAL

208 CHAPTER FIVE
"I TOOK AN OATH"

284 CHAPTER SIX
"IT'S NOT ABOUT ME"

330 CHAPTER SEVEN
MARKETING DOCTOR STRANGE

336 AFTERWORD
BY ALEXANDRA BYRNE

338 CONTRIBUTOR BIOS

340 ACKNOWLEDGMENTS

342 ARTIST CREDITS

*Who has a harder fight than he
who is striving to overcome himself?*
– Thomas à Kempis, 15th century Dutch mystic

In 1963, Stephen Strange first appeared in the anthology *Strange Tales*. He was a wild, unexpected left turn within the universe of Marvel Comics. Readers immediately responded so positively to the character that Strange was soon given his own unique origin story and then his own comic-book title. Those Stan Lee/Steve Ditko Doctor Strange comics increasingly represented the 1960s counterculture with progressive mystical ideas, alternate realities, and mind-expanding psychedelic imagery. Marvel Comics would never be the same.

When first meeting with Marvel Studios about possibly directing *Doctor Strange*, I told them that a film adaptation had to be a similarly wild left turn within the Marvel Cinematic Universe. It needed to be a bold journey into ideological mysticism, with daring visual ambition that utilized expensive visual effects to give audiences something more than tentpole set pieces of typical mass destruction. It had to be *psychedelic*. The goal was always to make a magical, mystical, mind-bending action film about one man overcoming himself. A film both epic and intimate—with huge, surreal set pieces highlighting the personal journey of Stephen Strange from a selfish, materialistic skeptic, through a gauntlet of trauma and loss, into the discovery of magic, self-denial, and spiritual transcendence. The origin story of a super-hero sorcerer.

The tone of my past work in the horror genre was dark. Those films were about the supernatural, but they were each grounded by real characters in the real world. That creative instinct—to keep one foot in the material world and the other in the supernatural—connects my previous films to Doctor Strange. And while I always thought that this movie would be both tonally and visually darker than past Marvel Studios films, I also knew it would be a mistake to make it too dark or overly self-serious. Tonally, it needed to be a kind of dark lite.

My process of making the movie began and ended with four extraordinary people at Marvel: Producer Kevin Feige, a proper genius; and executive producers Louis D'Esposito, Stephen Broussard, and Victoria Alonso, each as kind and decent as they are talented. We all made this film together. These four are not studio executives—they are gifted artists without egos, doing everything possible to service one thing: the film itself. Marvel Studios' outstanding track record is the result of their true love for cinema. They work from a single, pure motive—one perfectly stated by Walt Disney himself: "We don't make movies to make money, we make money to make more movies."

The scriptwriting process began with myself, Stephen Broussard, and Jon Spaihts breaking the story together. Jon wrote an excellent first draft, after which I took over along with my writing partner C. Robert Cargill. During the editorial phase, Jon came back to write a few additional photography scenes. The process was so synergistic, I couldn't tell you which parts of the script came from which writer.

The look of the film is primarily the result of a wonderfully complex collaboration between myself and the following key crew individuals: Marvel Head of Visual Development Ryan Meinerding, Director of Photography Ben Davis, Production Designer Charles Wood, Visual Effects Supervisor Stéphane Ceretti, and Costume Designer Alexandra Byrne. Each of them are amongst the best in the world at what they do, and each made the work process an absolute joy.

In both the comics and the film, Strange's traumatic accident forces him to reckon with himself in a way he never would have without the career-ending loss of his hands. This concept of personal growth through trauma and loss is at the heart of *Doctor Strange*. As is, of course, the notion of selflessness, best stated in what the Ancient One calls "the simplest and most significant lesson of them all..."

It's not about you.

Scott Derrickson

INTRODUCTION
THE IMPOSSIBILITIES ARE ENDLESS...

Stephen Vincent Strange—or as his friends (and enemies) more commonly call him, Doctor Strange—first appeared in issue #110 of the comic-book anthology *Strange Tales* in the summer of 1963.

Created by writer Stan Lee and artist Steve Ditko, Strange was already the sentient-cloak-wearing, rune-shield-wielding, all-powerful sorcerer readers know today—but as with most heroes in the Marvel Universe, his ascension was born from tragedy.

The brilliant Strange was once a preeminent neurosurgeon—possibly the world's best. It was a mantle he wore proudly—too proudly, some would say: Arrogance tended to overshadow his skill at saving lives. A car accident changed his overconfident tune when colleagues informed him that the nerve damage in his hands would prevent him from performing surgery ever again. Unable to swallow his pride, Strange began to search the globe for a way to restore his physical capabilities. The journey took him east, where he came face-to-face with the Ancient One, a timeless Master of the Mystic Arts. After proving his worth and casting aside his selfish tendencies, Strange immersed himself in the world of sorcery in an attempt to understand and harness the power of the mystic arts.

With their surreal visuals and increasingly unconventional storylines, the Doctor Strange stories in *Strange Tales* soon became cult favorites among comic-book readers, the rise in popularity cementing the character's importance in the Marvel Universe. As one of the most powerful sorcerers in existence, his feats of heroism were boundless. In addition to possessing telekinetic abilities and brandishing ancient relics of unfathomable power, he could manipulate the universe's ambient magical energy, project energy bolts, teleport, travel through time, and maneuver between dimensions.

By 1965—in a massive, 17-issue arc culminating in *Strange Tales #146*—Ditko's art had become even weirder and wilder, with the maniacal, multicolored dimensions in illustrations that resembled the abstract work of artists such as Salvador Dalí. But as the 1960s came to an end, the appeal of this bold, New Age, oftentimes outlandish character began to dwindle. Strange would go through waves of interest, while at other times only turning up in the role of supporting character—guest-starring in other heroes' titles; and serving as a teammate of Hulk, Sub-Mariner, and Silver Surfer in the pages of *Defenders*.

In the late '80s and early '90s, Strange returned to the limelight. He was once again headlining his own series—*Doctor Strange, Sorcerer Supreme*, which from 1988 to 1996—when he appeared in 1991's *Infinity Gauntlet* blockbuster event to help Adam Warlock and Earth's heroes take down Thanos and save the universe. In the

A different kind of super hero makes the scene, from *Strange Tales #110* (1963), written by Stan Lee and illustrated by Steve Ditko.

Art from *Strange Tales #138 (1965)*, by Steve Ditko.

course of the 90-issue run of *Doctor Strange, Sorcerer Supreme*, he lost the mantle of Earth's Sorcerer Supreme, learned chaos magic, and then eventually gained back his title. In 1993, Strange founded a new team featuring a rotating roster of heroes in *Secret Defenders*. But the character wasn't breaking new ground as in the Lee/Ditko days; he soon fell back into his niche role.

Brian K. Vaughan and Marcos Martin's *Doctor Strange: The Oath* rekindled the character's popularity in 2006. An exploration of Strange as a man, as a wizard, and as a physician, the limited series grounded the concept of Doctor Strange but never lost sight of the character's metaphysical roots as introduced by Lee and Ditko. The series also teed up Strange for inclusion in *New Avengers*, and set the standard for his appearances moving forward in the Marvel Universe.

Limitless in its potential, Stephen Strange's unconventional journey is a perfect fit for translation into the Marvel Cinematic Universe. "I've been talking about Doctor Strange for many, many years," Marvel Studios President Kevin Feige says. "It's been something that we've wanted to do for a long time because it represents a fresh, new aspect to the ever-expanding cinematic universe. Just like in the comics, *Doctor Strange* deals with parallel dimensions, alternate dimensions, and the Multiverse—which ultimately unlocks an entirely new era of storytelling for us."

Marvel Studios enlisted Director Scott Derrickson to helm the Sorcerer Supreme's origin story. "Scott Derrickson had a very unique vision—a sort of twisted sensibility—and can take a lot of these concepts and make them unbelievably visual and unbelievably, enthusiastically over the top and exciting," Feige says.

Breathing life into Stephen Strange was never going to be easy, but Derrickson embraced the challenge. "I think what we've seen happen within the Marvel Cinematic Universe is this ever-expanding clique of super heroes, and from that everything kind of blossoming out into the more surreal, the more extraordinary—so that you can then have wormholes in New York; you can have otherworldly destruction happening in this world's space and time," Derrickson says. "I think now we're at the stage where this universe, even within our world, has gotten quite crowded. It's just about to explode into other dimensions. You've had Thanos, who's already sort of rumbled in the background a little bit. I think Strange is a very natural bridge between what we know of New York or what we know of our sensual, sensory, perceivable reality, and something well beyond that."

Crafting a story that integrated the comics' distinctly ethereal qualities while maintaining a grounded, character-driven foundation was the first step. "Strange's origin is a challenging one in terms of places that we wanted to go with his journey," Executive Producer Stephen Broussard says. "Places you've never been before with our characters. Places that are Earthbound; places that are not. Mind-bending, transformative settings that, ideally, audiences will be unprepared for. That's the ambition."

While the script was coming together, Production Designer Charles Wood, Costume Designer Alexandra Byrne, Marvel Studios Head of Visual Development Ryan Meinerding, and Visual Effects Supervisor Stéphane Ceretti began a year-long conceptualization process to help realize the multifaceted world of *Doctor Strange*.

One of the film's key features would be an evolution of color. "When I first read the comics, I thought: This is madness," Byrne says. "Then you start taking it apart, breaking it down, digesting what it means and what it could become. We started to get bits of the script that were really grounding it in a tactile world. You begin to just chip away at the story, and decide on the visual language for the film and what the rules of the film are going to be—more specifically, what the visual rules are going to be. I think in the realm of *Doctor Strange*, color is really important. All of the departments banded together and worked very closely on the journey of color through the film."

"We wanted to produce a film that really had a signature to it, had a look—bold, but also following a path," Wood says. "So as we set out, I would continually think back to words that Scott always said to me: He wanted a film that was very rich, dark, and luminous. 'Luminous' was a lovely word; it led the way for an idea—that sense of color, light, reflection, and such we could add into a lot of these kinds of dreamy worlds. A lot of the spaces we produced are quite graphic, as well. It was based on a comic, so we're always trying to strive for imagery that's strong—not so much colorful, but rich. That sort of segues into these dreamy realms."

The filmmakers also faced the challenge of representing the scope of magic in the Marvel Cinematic Universe. Marvel's *Thor* revealed that magic was simply science not yet understood—meaning that as a doctor, Stephen Strange was already a magician of sorts. What *Thor* didn't explore was the implementation of magic—its rules, uses, and repercussions—which Strange comes to learn during his time with the Ancient One at her school, the Kamar-Taj. "When we first met with Scott, he had already compiled a set of images he found inspiring," Ceretti says. "He wanted to make magic feel real—in the sense that it was reliable, it was practical, it was physical. Scott and I looked at long-exposure photography of sparks and pyrotechnics, images that created circles and shapes from the light. There was an optical and physical feel to it, as if it was tangible. This lead to what Scott called the Eldritch magic, which is the magic the students at the Kamar-Taj are conjuring. The Eldritch magic can be shaped into weapons like fans or whips, but can also be used defensively to form shields—much like you see in the comic books. While we focused on keeping the magic physical, we were cautious in trying to stay away from anything that felt wispy or overly particle-based."

In the films of the Marvel Cinematic Universe, the "super" elements are always supplementary to the "hero" moments—and *Doctor Strange* would be no exception. "He is a fascinating character because he has a wonderful arc in the story," Broussard says. "When we first find him in the film, he's dark, he's brooding, he's complex. He has gone down a path that anyone could go down in the mistakes we all make in life. Then tragedy strikes him, and he has to confront himself. Amid the visual effects and spectacle, there's a nice human quality to the film."

Benedict Cumberbatch, who plays the titular character, was the first choice for the role. "I found him incredibly arrogant, brilliant, sort of extraordinary, and with a potential to be incredibly hokey because it was very much a comic of its era, like they always are," Cumberbatch says. "This super hero came out of a context of the '60s and '70s

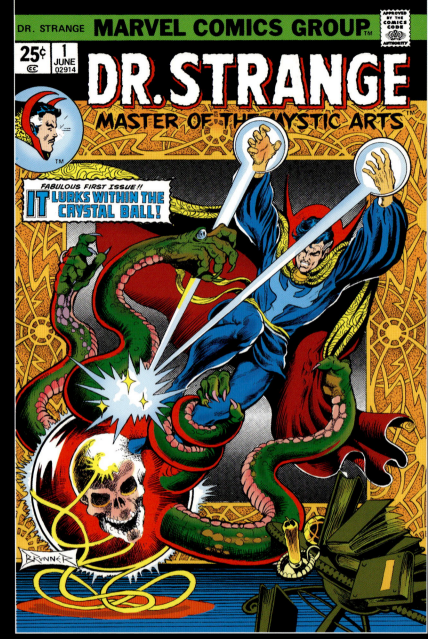

Cover to *Doctor Strange #1 (1974)*, by Frank Brunner.

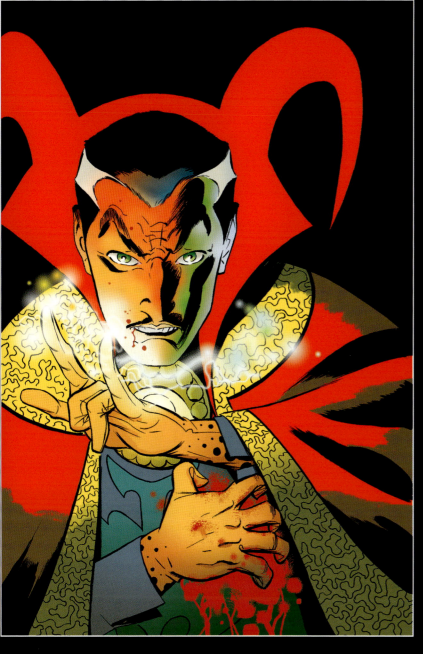

Cover to *Doctor Strange: The Oath #1 (2006)*, by Marcos Martin.

bleed between western science and logic and eastern mysticism—which is something as a teenager I was very interested in.

"I spent some time teaching in a Tibetan Buddhist monastery near Darjeeling, as well as studying Buddhist texts, reading up on certain things, and observing this extraordinary ancient ritual and wisdom right in front of me every morning and every evening—talking to monks in that monastery, talking to lamas in the towns about who had experiences with other sects or had better English. They were very able to sort of unpack what I was witnessing every day.

"My mind, as a 19-year-old, was kind of really blown open by all of that. So it immediately made sense to me, this material. My fear initially was that because the comics are very, very out there, how does this concept work? Why would this concept work in the 21st century? What is it about this character that would grip us now? And beyond him being a bridge into other-dimensional threats and worlds and battles, and kind of broadening the scope of the Marvel Cinematic Universe—as an actor, why do we all want to do this project now? It was mainly the character arc and the journey he goes on in the film that drew me to the material. He goes on this massive journey of self-discovery and is utterly crushed. He has to suffer humility after humility after humility—it's very different from the comics in that extent. He's utterly broken down to be reconstituted into the super hero who then is fully fledged by the end of this movie. There's a lot of humor on the way; there's a lot of action, a lot of drama. All those elements really, really appeal to me as an actor."

"We have a cast that, I think, has more awards and more award nominations than any single cast we've ever put together," Feige says. "And the fact that they're all willing to suit up, to step into this very trippy world with us, is a testament to both our director Scott Derrickson and the source material that it comes from. This is a mind trip that rivals any that has ever been done before. We have the technology now to take what Steve Ditko created back in the '60s and put that into three-dimensional space on a movie screen—and we're not pulling back. The Cinematic Universe has thrived for us at Marvel Studios when we just take what was great about the comics, and unabashedly and without fear throw it up on the big screen. There are images and sequences in *Doctor Strange* that people have already been calling the most breathtaking sort of mind trip that they've ever seen in a movie before. That was our challenge, and that's what we think the team has risen to."

As the 14th installment in the Marvel Cinematic Universe, *Doctor Strange* is ushering in a new era of filmmaking in terms of both scope and technical prowess—as well as expanding the ever-evolving world for future Marvel properties.

CHAPTER ONE
TRAGEDY AND REBIRTH

A tragic childhood event instills within Stephen Strange a need to control fate, to manipulate destiny—to conquer death—and that obsession carries him to the height of his profession as a neurosurgeon. But Strange's pursuit of wealth, social status, and professional recognition eventually supersedes his goal of saving lives. He rejects cases that don't interest him or won't further his career. All of that changes when bad luck sends his car—and his future—careening into a ditch.

"I think it's so unexpected, what happens to him in that moment with the car crash," actor Benedict Cumberbatch says. "You immediately see everything in that person's world disappear in a matter of seconds—everything.

"You see him as a lone figure at the beginning and end of this film. By the end of the film, he's a super hero, and we all know that's quite an onerous task and often a solitary existence. There aren't too many people you can pillow-talk or form meaningful relationships with when your responsibilities are always other and elsewhere. Strange suffers so much during the film—not just physically, but psychologically."

After a series of failed surgical procedures, attempting to salvage the damaged nerves in his hands leaves him with a dwindling bank account, Strange heads east to Kathmandu—where a mysterious healer awaits.

Pete Thompson concept art.

THE ACCIDENT

Pete Thompson concept art.

"Doctor Strange has probably the best solo origin story of any Marvel character," Marvel Studios President Kevin Feige says. "He is an incredibly talented, incredibly arrogant neurosurgeon at the top of his game in Manhattan, and he does not have the best bedside manner; he is more interested in taking cases in which he can push his own ego, in which he can push his own reputation so that he can get his name up on the side of hospital wings devoted to his expertise. It is while he is taking a car ride to one of these unveilings of his name on yet another wing of a building that he gets into a car accident. And his hands—what he believes are his true gift, the reason he can do the kinds of operations that he does—are completely mangled."

CHAPTER ONE: TRAGEDY AND REBIRTH

Early in the development process, the filmmakers considered forgoing Doctor Strange's origin story. But for Director Scott Derrickson, part of what makes Strange a compelling character is the emotional resonance of his history.

"There's a little bit of a backlash that I've sensed from fans of comic-book movies about origin stories, but I think every movie with a good character is an origin story—whether it's a comic-book movie or not," Derrickson says. "It's a story about how they became the person they are at the end of the movie. And I think that in this instance, the origin story of Stephen Strange is uniquely good. We talked about possibly not showing it and really just meeting him as Doctor Strange, Master of the Mystic Arts, and telling the tale that we have to tell without delving into that aspect of him, and it just felt like a mistake. It felt like you'd be shortchanging the richness of that character to not know who he was prior to his exposure to sorcery. Honestly, a lot of the movie has nothing to do with that original origin story of a car crash and mangled hands and how he comes upon the Ancient One and is introduced to sorcery. There's a lot more to it than just that, but I'm incredibly excited that it's part of the movie, because that's part of what I love about Doctor Strange. If you don't know him as the arrogant, wealthy, skeptical, materialistic man of hubris that he was, you really can't appreciate the man he becomes—the gravity and the responsibility he comes to accept in his life."

Jackson Sze concept art.

Pete Thompson concept art.

"I always like painting character-driven, emotional moments," Head of Visual Development Ryan Meinerding says. "This image was done fairly early on and was about showcasing Stephen Strange after he lost the thing he considers to be his identity: his hands. It gave me the opportunity to explore a quiet, emotional frame—an image about loss and isolation."

Ryan Meinerding keyframe.

KATHMANDU, NEPAL

Kamar-Taj, school of the mystic arts and residence of the Ancient One, is located in the heart of Nepal: Kathmandu. "The textures in this city are so unique we realized that we couldn't just do a green screen and background plates," Executive Producer Stephen Broussard says. "We had to immerse the character here in the city to make this part of his journey, which is an amazing journey for his transformation from Dr. Stephen Strange into the character he ultimately becomes in the movie. Just being there, you can see the textures, the feelings, the smells: They all give the actor that much more to work with—and then for Scott Derrickson, the director, to work with, too."

Roberto Fernández Castro concept art.

"We scouted Kathmandu in the fall of 2014, and shortly thereafter there was a cataclysmic earthquake," Executive Producer Charles Newirth says. "We had fallen in love with the city and the people. There was a real concern: Would it be safe for us to go there? Is the studio going to feel comfortable for us to go there? We had tremendous concern for the people of Kathmandu. Some time went by, and we felt it was the right thing to do. I was a little nervous that we were not going to be able to go back there. But we convinced the studio. And they felt comfortable enough to let us go back.

It was a number of months later that we ended up being on the streets of Kathmandu.

It'd be very, very difficult to find another city that would sit in and replicate the spirituality, the architecture, the special quality that Kathmandu was bringing us in the film. The people there opened their hearts and their homes and their businesses and their squares to us. We worked in an environment where you could still see the remnants of the destruction that happened a number of months before. But these people are so unique and so beautiful that they've gone on with their lives. And that in and of itself, I think, touched every crew member. I know it touched me."

CHAPTER ONE: TRAGEDY AND REBIRTH

Roberto Fernández Castro concept art.

"Kathmandu was absolutely vital to this film," Benedict Cumberbatch says. "It was incredibly important that we as a representative of a very big global franchise went there to do our work and to appreciate the people and culture of Nepal. For that to be shown on screen, for that to be real, for them as much as for us—I was incredibly relieved and grateful when it all worked out. It was a magical way to start the shoot. It was mind-boggling—a beautiful, beautiful city, with beautiful people. They'd been through so much. Months after the earthquake damage, there were still shantytowns that we'd pass every day. You could see the devastation in some of the most famous tourist spots. At Patan Durbar Square, one of the places we filmed in, you could see where temples had been destroyed or partially damaged or affected in some way by the earthquake. Slightly outside of Kathmandu, the shock was a lot bigger. The damage was a lot more prevalent—entirely flattened areas of farmland, villages, or ancient town squares. And yet there was such resilience. It was incredibly inspiring."

CHAPTER ONE: TRAGEDY AND REBIRTH

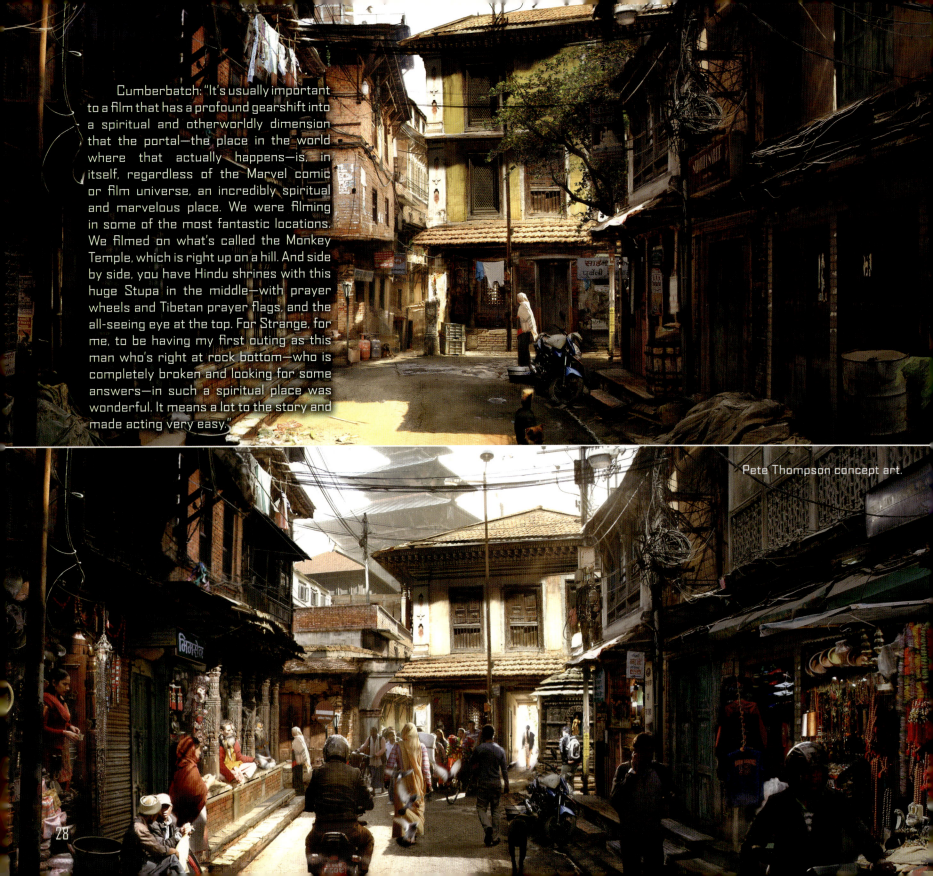

Cumberbatch: "It's usually important to a film that has a profound gearshift into a spiritual and otherworldly dimension that the portal—the place in the world where that actually happens—is, in itself, regardless of the Marvel comic or film universe, an incredibly spiritual and marvelous place. We were filming in some of the most fantastic locations. We filmed on what's called the Monkey Temple, which is right up on a hill. And side by side, you have Hindu shrines with this huge Stupa in the middle—with prayer wheels and Tibetan prayer flags, and the all-seeing eye at the top. For Strange, for me, to be having my first outing as this man who's right at rock bottom—who is completely broken and looking for some answers—in such a spiritual place was wonderful. It means a lot to the story and made acting very easy."

Pete Thompson concept art.

Pete Thompson concept art.

Roberto Fernández Castro concept art.

CHAPTER ONE: TRAGEDY AND REBIRTH

Concept Artist Jackson Sze painted a number of atmospheric images to inspire him as he began to try to capture the film's essence. "This keyframe was a time-based concept showing how you can view two different realities at once," Sze says. "Essentially, the elements in the foreground, including Strange, are in the present, and behind the rippling, prism-like colors is the same environment many, many years in the future—as you can see with the elements of overgrowth. It wasn't necessarily a script-based beat—it was more about capturing the moment of experience pertaining to time differences in a single frame."

Jackson Sze concept art.

KAMAR-TAJ CENTRAL COMPOUND

In the comics, Kamar-Taj is located deep in the mountains, far from any semblance of civilization. The filmmakers sought to step away from the well-worn trope, instead placing the school right in the center of Kathmandu. Once shooting in Nepal wrapped, Production Designer Charles Wood oversaw construction of the school's ornate interiors on a soundstage in London.

"The Kamar-Taj was a series of sets we built based on what we found in Kathmandu," Wood says. "We did a few days of filming in Kathmandu, where we filmed Benedict in some of the temples and on some of the streets; then you sort of end up going round the corner, and you end up in Longcross—on a soundstage. That's tricky. It's hard because Kathmandu is a beautiful city. It's steeped in history. It's many millennia old. To transition from that level of detail, that level of history—the shape of the streets, the warping of the buildings, these ancient bricks, these ancient tiles... It's a frenetic city. It's choking. It's extraordinary. It's colorful. It's mad. It's crazy. And to go round a corner and walk onto a street that is still connected to Kathmandu was a real challenge."

Roberto Fernández Castro concept art.

"I've been all over the world, but there's no place on the planet like Kathmandu," Scott Derrickson says. "It is a city with virtually no Western influence in it—it's 85 percent Hindu and 15 percent Tibetan Buddhist. It is a large city that is so deeply mystical and religious in all operations—but in the most peaceful, beautiful, colorful way. It's an impoverished country, but there's a beauty and a peace to that place that was so surprising to me, and the visual qualities of that city are unlike anywhere else. They just are. There's no place in the world that looks like Kathmandu, and so we'd liked the idea anyway, but after going there it just seemed like we had chosen something that was far better than we even imagined it would be."

Roberto Fernández Castro concept art.

CHAPTER ONE: TRAGEDY AND REBIRTH

"After visiting Kathmandu, I told Charlie, 'I want windows everywhere! I want to be seeing out into the city all the time!' That way we're not bound to the insides, and the presence of the actual city itself is always visible."

The seamless melding of Wood's extravagant set and the outside world of Kathmandu was left in the hands of the Visual Effects team. "Using the rough measurements of the Kamar-Taj, we shot helicopter plates in Kathmandu that, in conjunction with photography we did on the ground there, would serve as reference to recreate the city in 3-D," Visual Effects Supervisor Stéphane Ceretti says. "The vendor we're using, Method, took all of the reference and created an incredibly detailed and authentic view of the surrounding city to use while we're on the rooftops of the Kamar-Taj."

Roberto Fernández Castro concept art.

"Almost everything seen in the courtyard and sanctuary sets is in-camera—no visual effects," Visual Effects Producer Susan Pickett says. "The walls were 20 to 25 feet high, and we extended the set digitally beyond that, but everything that's happening in most of the sequences is in-camera. It's truly a testament to the level of intricacy and research that Charles Wood and his entire team use to fabricate the designs that translate into these sets."

Roberto Fernández Castro concept art.

"You really had to feel this place being around for a few centuries," Wood says. "I hope to produce sets that would make an audience feel that the Ancient One really existed in this place. That it was truly spiritual, truly magical, and was truly on top of a building that we photographed in Kathmandu that actually existed there. That's always where you want to end up."

Roberto Fernández Castro concept art.

Pete Thompson concept art.

SLING RINGS

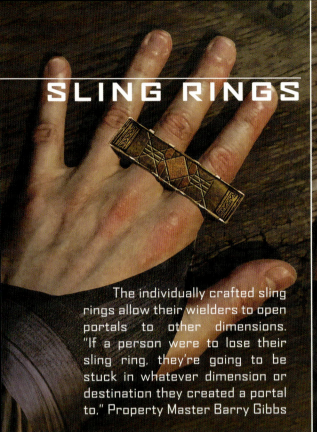

The individually crafted sling rings allow their wielders to open portals to other dimensions. "If a person were to lose their sling ring, they're going to be stuck in whatever dimension or destination they created a portal to," Property Master Barry Gibbs

says. "We explored a number of different looks to try and create a balanced look of antiquity and power without letting them get too flashy or gaudy. We're never really seeing them that close up, but we still want them to have an interesting read—even from a distance."

DOCTOR STRANGE

THE ANCIENT ONE

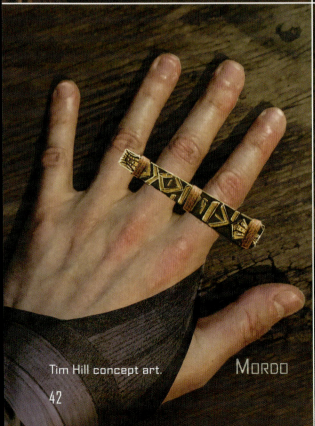

Tim Hill concept art.

MORDO

KAECILIUS

KAMAR-TAJ TRAINEE

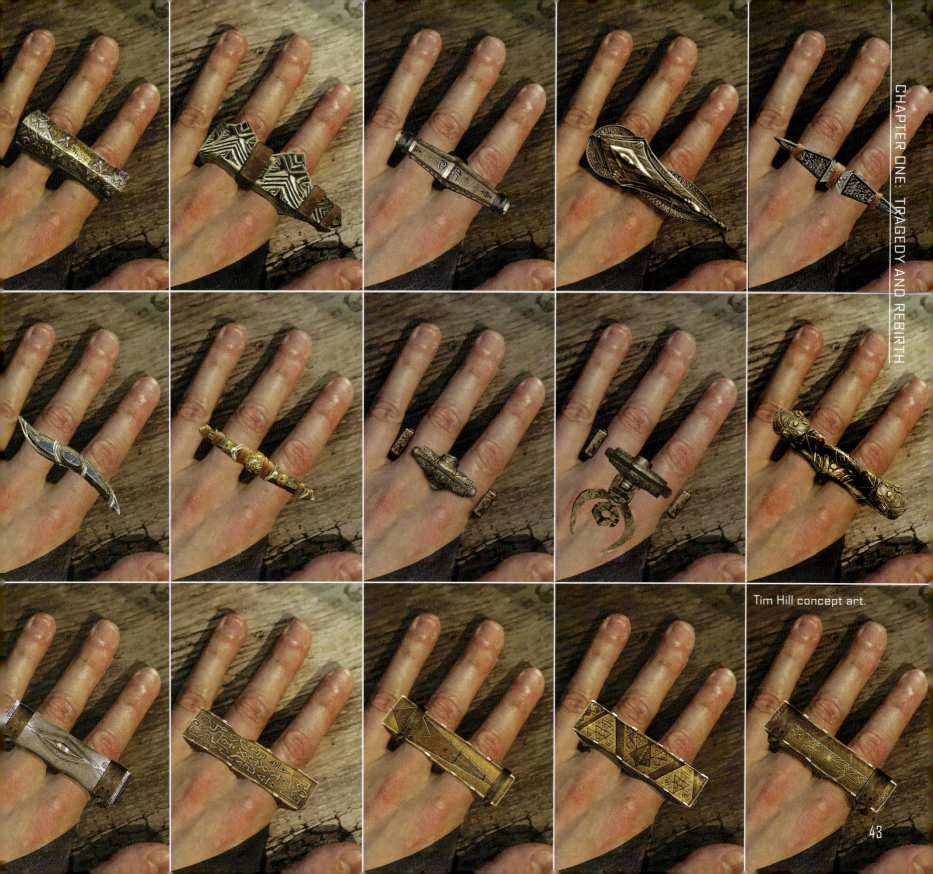

CHAPTER ONE: TRAGEDY AND REBIRTH

Tim Hill concept art.

KAMAR-TAJ NOVICES

Jack Dudman concept art.

KAMAR-TAJ APPRENTICES

To visually divide the ranks of students at the Kamar-Taj, Costume Designer Alexandra Byrne created a color system that defines their roles—white for novices, burgundy for apprentices, and blue for disciples—while the looks for the masters are tailored to the characters' personalities. "Although the Kamar-Taj clothes are about this ancient mysticism, the clothes are very real," Byrne says. "They're dirty. They're worn. They've got repairs on them. I think to support the magic, you actually also have to have a reality."

Jack Dudman concept art.

KAMAR-TAJ DISCIPLES

Jack Dudman concept art.

Kan Muftic concept art.

For Byrne, maintaining a sense of reality meant balancing practicality with elegance—for the sake of not only the film's believability, but also the needs of the actors and crew. "They've got to fight in them. They've got to run in them. They've got to somersault in them. They've got to fly in them. They have to be able to move in every way," she says. "This isn't a period film that is about a starlet moving around in flashy clothes—it's all about martial arts. The joy of this film is that unlike all the other Marvel films I've done, there is no Lycra involved, anywhere. The clothes are made to be moving—and so they do."

Kan Muftic concept art.

CHAPTER ONE: TRAGEDY AND REBIRTH

MORDO

In the comics, Mordo is to Doctor Strange what Moriarty is to Sherlock Holmes: a highly skilled, equal adversary. The archvillain's origin is surprisingly similar to Strange's: Mordo is a former disciple of the Ancient One who, despite his great skill, was corrupted by greed and pride.

"What's interesting to me about Mordo is not what's in the comics, but what you infer about him as you read through them, which was: He wasn't always this guy," Scott Derrickson says. "He was somebody who came in and was a good student, and had tremendous capabilities as a sorcerer, and had good qualities—along with the qualities that draw him into evil. I wanted to be able to take time in this movie to introduce Mordo as the good character that he is. He's almost like Lucifer in Paradise Lost or Michael Corleone in The Godfather: one of these characters who starts off as the epitome of quality, goodness, and beauty, and you get to incrementally see him make decisions that take him down a path—and at what point does he really cross the line? It's almost hard to say because his decisions seem so justified all along the way, and yet he does find himself connected to Dormammu—and completely seduced by absolute, antihuman evil."

Ryan Meinerding concept art.

Jack Dudman concept art.

CHAPTER ONE: TRAGEDY AND REBIRTH

For Mordo's costume, Ryan Meinerding built upon the design for the Kamar-Taj masters. "One of the more challenging things about adapting Marvel villains is that they tend to have a green-and-yellow color scheme. We've done it a couple times with Loki and the Mandarin," Meinerding says. "Once Alex [Byrne] had figured out the rough idea for the progression of students through the Kamar-Taj, the masters' rank offered the opportunity for each character to be slightly unique. So we looked in the comics for places to incorporate the signature green, but deviated slightly so it didn't feel like we were really resorting back to the same color schemes we've used for villains before. I was trying to bring in the green with more of a cream color, as well as other colors like purple and deep blue. Also, since robes are often symmetrical in a very specific way, I tried to bring some asymmetry to the robe and how it wraps around his waist, as well as the asymmetry on his arm. The asymmetry was a visual way to allude to the imbalance of Mordo's character."

Anthony Francisco concept art.

"I wanted to accentuate an intricate, woven feel, as [Mordo is] a very intricate character," Concept Artist Anthony Francisco says. "When doing character designs, I try to tell myself a story, and I try to use symbolism within my design to express personality. The emblem was something I also wanted to subtly tie in. It's part of his icon. Materials were a big part of the Mordo look, too—soft materials, weaving with cloth, no hard pieces. Staying away from things that feel too modern. Lots of layering, at first, but in the end we went with a more form-fitting look."

Anthony Francisco concept art.

"I started my character designs with a gray background because it's simple, but I had to put some light in there to make it feel more...magical. It really adds to the presentation. With the purple backgrounds, it's more about creating contrast so the green could feel more green. Once I started doing more illustration stuff where the storytelling was a big part, I wanted to add some story in, so I utilized the setting where he does his magic and training. It gives him a more authentic feel when you start putting him in an environment where it feels he belongs, where the costume could have originated from."

Anthony Francisco concept art.

Karla Ortiz concept art.

"[Mordo is] one of the masters of the Kamar-Taj," Alexandra Byrne says. "So that's the most important part costume-wise, and then his story takes off from there. I don't want to dress his story—I want to dress his origin."

Anthony Francisco concept art.

KAMAR-TAJ MASTER TINA MINORU

Kan Muftic concept art.

KAMAR-TAJ MASTER SOL RAMA

CHAPTER ONE: TRAGEDY AND REBIRTH

Jack Dudman concept art.

55

KAMAR-TAJ MASTER DANIEL DRUMM

Jack Dudman concept art.

KAMAR-TAJ RUNES

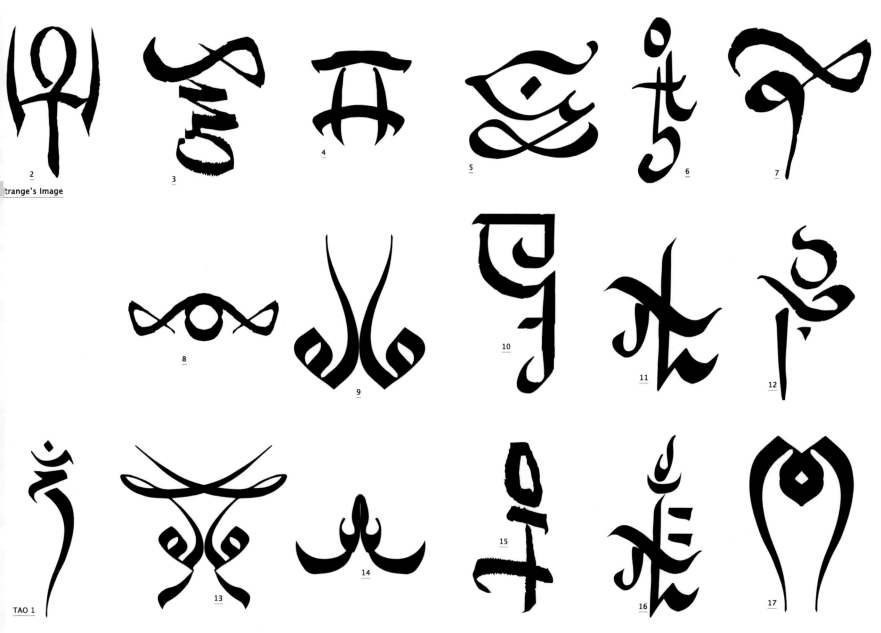

Anna Haigh concept art.

THE ANCIENT ONE

"One of the biggest challenges in the movie, casting-wise, was the Ancient One," Scott Derrickson says. "The idea of the wizened old man on the hill who becomes the one who bequeaths knowledge and insight and all of that is a kind of cliché by now. Yet the Ancient One is so critical to the Doctor Strange mythology, you have to have the Ancient One, and you have to make the Ancient One alive and real and interesting and three-dimensional. I struggled so hard in both coming up with the story and working on the screenplay, but then when it came to casting, I was even feeling more befuddled by what we can do that's not going to end up feeling like a trope of some sort. The starting point was, 'What if it's a woman?' You know, why can't it be? You know already the idea that the Ancient One is the head of all sorcerers; now that person is also a woman. I'm already interested, and I'm already feeling liberated from the chains of cliché."

Jack Dudman concept art.

Anthony Francisco concept art.

Kan Muftic concept art.

CHAPTER ONE: TRAGEDY AND REBIRTH

The Ancient One's look went through a number of iterations—some based in sheer simplicity, others reflecting a more grandiose nature—all of which highlighted various facets of the character as she evolved with the script and the decision to cast actress and fashion icon Tilda Swinton. "Obviously, I started with the comics and the mood boards and went through that process," Alexandra Byrne says. "Then we were drawing. When Tilda came on board, that's a huge casting input because Tilda has basically done almost every style of fashion shoot. So what we didn't want is for it to look like Tilda styled as the Ancient One. We wanted to find a language that was very particular and true to the character and maybe not sensationalist, so that it had a kind of a gravitas to it—and a simplicity. I think that's all about setting up very subtle contradictions and nuances within the costume, rather than it being a big kind of hole-in-one kind of hit. So Tilda and I worked very closely. That was also understanding and developing the walk, the posture, the style of fighting, working very closely with [Makeup Designer] Jeremy [Woodhead] because how she looks in her face and her hair, that's all very important: It's about the sum of information that you're bringing to the character."

Anthony Francisco concept art.

Kan Muftic concept art.

CHAPTER ONE: TRAGEDY AND REBIRTH

The Ancient One's gender swap gave Concept Artist Jerad Marantz the opportunity to explore a wide range of designs for the character. "We were working on her while also trying to figure out the general look for the Kamar-Taj students," Marantz says. "It was very early on. The biggest design issue was trying to figure out how Tilda would influence the character. Would her femininity play into the costume design, or would she be more androgynous? The concepts that I was doing explored that range."

Jerad Marantz concept art.

Jerad Marantz concept art.

CHAPTER ONE: TRAGEDY AND REBIRTH

63

TAO FIGHTING MANDALA

"We worked with this extraordinary stunt team," Tilda Swinton says. "We worked with martial artists, obviously—people like Vincent Wong, who's a genius of Chinese martial arts. We've also been working with J-Funk [martial artist and dancer Julian Daniels], who taught us all these extraordinary tutting moves with our hands. It was a technical issue about getting us ready to be in front of the camera doing these things in an authoritative way. It was like being back at school. We were learning all these things that we would never otherwise have learned."

Kan Muftic concept art.

Jack Dudman concept art.

CHAPTER ONE: TRAGEDY AND REBIRTH

TAO MANDALAS

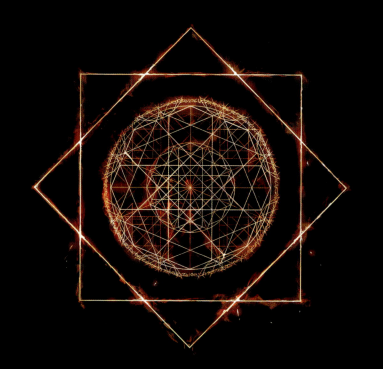

Bob Cheshire concept art.

Bob Cheshire concept art.

CHAPTER ONE: TRAGEDY AND REBIRTH

TAO SANCTUARY

Roberto Fernández Castro concept art.

CHAPTER ONE: TRAGEDY AND REBIRTH

Pete Thompson concept art.

CHAPTER ONE: TRAGEDY AND REBIRTH

CHAPTER TWO
"EVER SEE THAT IN A GIFT SHOP?"

Ryan Lang keyframe.

As a man of reason, Stephen Strange initially fails to grasp the notion of space-time, of dimensions beyond the world he knows. The Ancient One encourages him to embrace an extended reality and thus begin his path to healing. When he rejects her advice, she forces Strange—and the audience—into what the filmmakers have dubbed the "Magical Mystery Tour."

"Apart from anything else, to be really specific, it's about creation," Tilda Swinton says. "It's about creativity. It's about the mind. It's about bending things—it's not about breaking things, if that makes sense. It's hallucinogenic. It's a trip for everybody in the film, not only for Stephen Strange. He's our avatar because he's the newbie. Similarly, the audience are newbies with him."

The Magical Mystery Tour is a visual exploration of what exists outside the world we know—an introduction to magic, parallel dimensions, and extraterrestrial threats that defy conventional wisdom.

"It's a very, very complex scene with a lot of people involved to make it work," Visual Effects Supervisor Stéphane Ceretti says. "We looked at tons of reference—from basic 'traveling through the universe' stuff, to macro photography, to fractal art—and using that, [Production Designer] Charlie [Wood] and [Marvel Studios Head of Visual Development] Ryan [Meinerding] had their artists produce a number of concepts on the different beats and essentially establish a visual storyline. It was a very long process to design the worlds—and then on top of that, we had to translate those designs into an action sequence that we conceptualized with a 3-D animatic by our pre-viz team."

FREE YOUR MIND

Strange's interdimensional journey forces him to free his mind, and Tilda Swinton hopes the audience will follow. "It feels to me like a huge experimental film," Swinton says. "And I don't know whether Marvel films always do feel like that. Maybe they do. But it feels like we're making a huge experimental film. And it's exciting. Everybody I know on the film who's made other Marvel films knows that it's slightly different. It's a mind trip."

Jackson Sze concept art.

"There's no real reference you can pull from because it's supposed to be an out-of-body, interdimensional experience, so I wanted to make it as trippy and as grand as we could—the goal being that it becomes a magical and mind-bending adventure for the audience," Concept Artist Jackson Sze says of these early keyframes. "The biggest challenge was determining, 'Is this unique enough?' It's got to be epic in scale. So continually reaching for that, while balancing the necessary storytelling elements, was a real challenge.

Jackson Sze concept art.

CHAPTER TWO: "EVER SEE THAT IN A GIFT SHOP?"

"I used an idea of what I thought had potential to be the visual look of the astral form. We knew that there was going to be a lot more research and development done down the line, so this was a combination of what I thought it could be and also what I could achieve in a timely manner to accommodate the development pipeline. I had a massive number of images to accomplish in a short period of time, so I needed a quick but interesting way to represent the astral form."

Jackson Sze concept art.

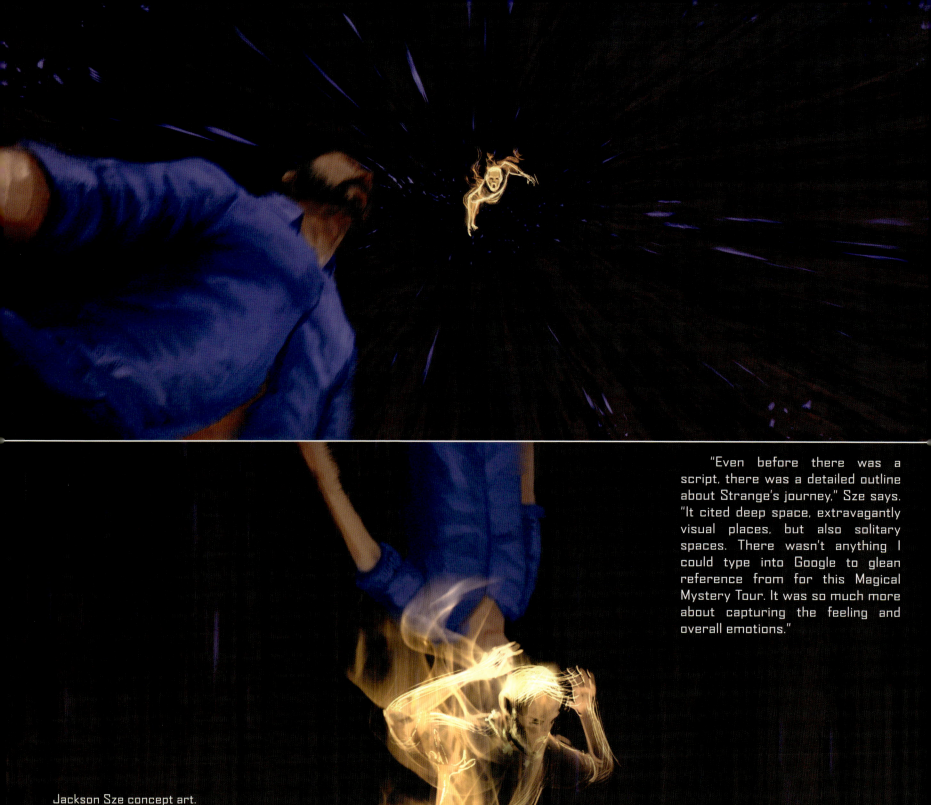

"Even before there was a script, there was a detailed outline about Strange's journey," Sze says. "It cited deep space, extravagantly visual places, but also solitary spaces. There wasn't anything I could type into Google to glean reference from for this Magical Mystery Tour. It was so much more about capturing the feeling and overall emotions."

Jackson Sze concept art.

CHAPTER TWO: "EVER SEE THAT IN A GIFT SHOP?"

Jackson Sze concept art.

In one of the story's early beats, Strange sees himself at various points in his life—past, present, and potential future. "To represent this multiple timeline of Doctor Strange, I knew the final product would be a combination of interesting visuals and the actor's performance," Sze says. "So I was honestly thinking the actor would sell that moment of seeing himself young and old in different possibilities across this timeline.

Jackson Sze concept art.

CHAPTER TWO: "EVER SEE THAT IN A GIFT SHOP?"

"As to what was required for each frame, I think it depends on what that moment called for. Was it an introspective personal moment? Or was it just Strange flying through space and experiencing fantastic environments? If it is more about himself, then the colors are way more subdued—it's all about Strange. It's more like a spotlight on him. Whereas if it's about the environment, it goes all-out color and crazy lines."

Jackson Sze concept art.

81

MIRROR DIMENSION

The Ancient One tells Strange of a separate reality, apart from the Astral Plane. Those within this Mirror Dimension remain on Earth, but their actions have no impact on the world outside. "To visualize this, we looked at what mirrors do and incorporated a kaleidoscopic feel into that," Stéphane Ceretti says. "We eventually created these 'mirror portals,' where the characters can go through these fracturing, mirror-like openings and end up in the Mirror Dimension. Like many of the high-concept ideas, it was continually evolving. There are things we came up with before the shoot and during the shoot, and then we continued to find new ideas and new devices to tell the story even in post-production."

Roberto Fernández Castro keyframe.

CHAPTER TWO: "EVER SEE THAT IN A GIFT SHOP?"

CHAPTER TWO: "EVER SEE THAT IN A GIFT SHOP?"

Roberto Fernández Castro keyframe.

85

Roberto Fernández Castro keyframe.

CHAPTER TWO: "EVER SEE THAT IN A GIFT SHOP?"

"Scott Derrickson has a great body of work," Marvel Studios President Kevin Feige says. "And like Joe and Anthony Russo, like Joss Whedon, like Jon Favreau, like Kenneth Branagh, the best of the filmmakers we've worked with haven't necessarily done a film like the one we're asking them to do now, but they've done enough that they've shown they're incredibly talented; they have unique visions and a love of film and a love of pushing the boundaries of what a movie can be. You look at Scott's work going back to the earliest days to his most recent films, he's always playing with the genre, he's always subverting the genre. Sometimes he dives right into it, sometimes he twists it—that's exactly what we love to do at Marvel."

Roberto Fernández Castro keyframe.

"You've got the whole world of Doctor Strange and New York and the hospitals that he's working in and his apartment where he lives and the car crash and what then happens to him afterwards—so that in itself has its own look," Production Designer Charles Wood says. "Then you've got this other world, the Magical Mystery Tour. It's like a series of paving stones you jump on. Then you jump onto the next and jump on the next. And you end up with this look from thousands of concept drawings. Then what you do is try and put it all together. You follow a color palette. You follow a structural palette. And you sort of build it over many months into a roadmap of how the film should look."

CHAPTER TWO: "EVER SEE THAT IN A GIFT SHOP?"

Roberto Fernández Castro keyframe.

89

Bob Cheshire keyframe.

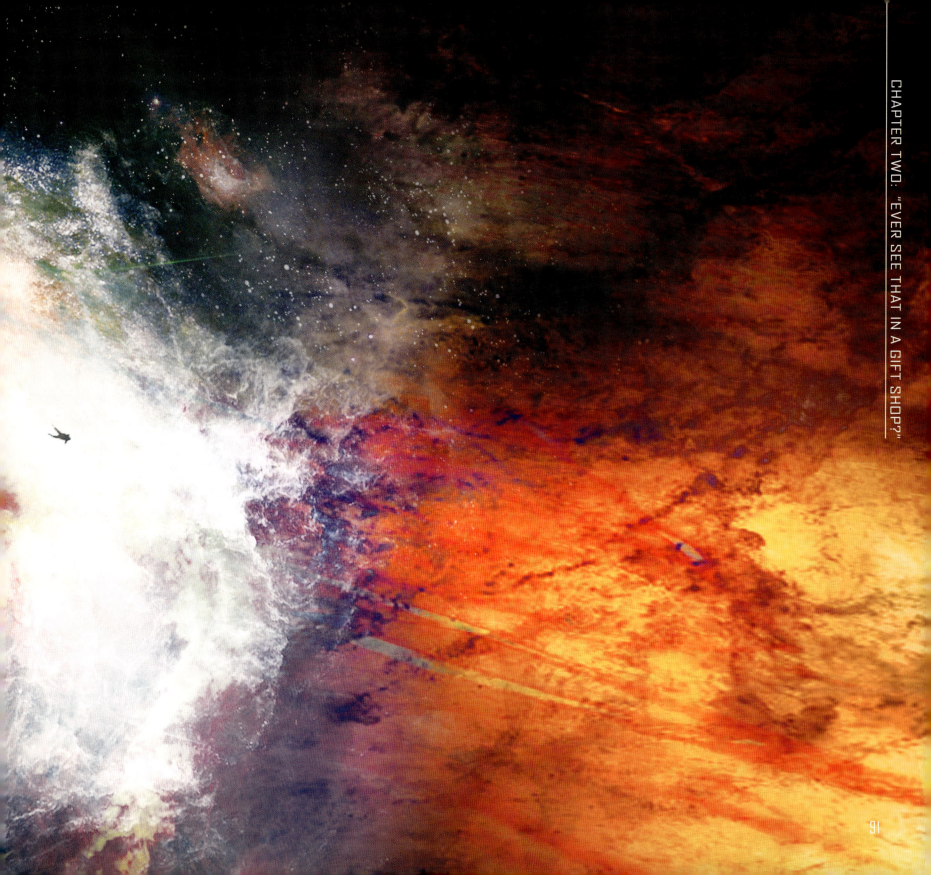

CHAPTER TWO: "EVER SEE THAT IN A GIFT SHOP?"

Roberto Fernández Castro keyframe.

Roberto Fernández Castro keyframe.

Pete Thompson keyframe.

CHAPTER TWO: "EVER SEE THAT IN A GIFT SHOP?"

"I do think *Doctor Strange* is one of those comics that artists love," Director Scott Derrickson says. "Creative people know that comic. Musicians know that comic. It's had a tremendous influence in roundabout ways all over the place, and I constantly see things where I just think, 'They had to have gotten that from *Strange* because I've never seen it anywhere else.' And yet there's still so much in the comics that you could never rip off because it only makes sense in the *Doctor Strange* universe."

Keyframe by Paul Chandler & Roberto Fernández Castro.

Roberto Fernández Castro keyframe.

"One of the things that's important to us in telling a magical story is keeping things within bounds, making sure that there's rules, making sure that you understand magic," Executive Producer Stephen Broussard says. "One of the great things about magic in storytelling is also one of the things that can be frustrating: that anything is a spell away from being solved. Any problem can just be solved very simply if you have magic on the table because magic fixes everything. So part of keeping it grounded and making sure that it exists within this world—and that it can stand alongside things like Iron Man that revolve around physics and mechanical engineering—is keeping it all in a box and understanding the rules and laying out the 'dos and don'ts' and the 'cans and can'ts' for our hero, but still leaving enough room to have fun."

Roberto Fernández Castro keyframe.

"I think the way to do that is that we're looking for a new way into magic. How do you explain magic in the Marvel Cinematic Universe in a way that you may not necessarily have seen before? When you think about magic in storytelling, you think about some of the greatest stories old and new that have been told that deal with sorcery. Harry Potter comes to mind, and Merlin, and the great sorcerers and the great wizards of literature and film. Knowing that's great and that we're probably not going to top it if we fight them at their own game, we're trying to come up with something completely different and have them exist in a magical realm that plays by its own rules, and is very specific to this movie and this character."

Roberto Fernández Castro keyframe.

Paul Catling keyframe.

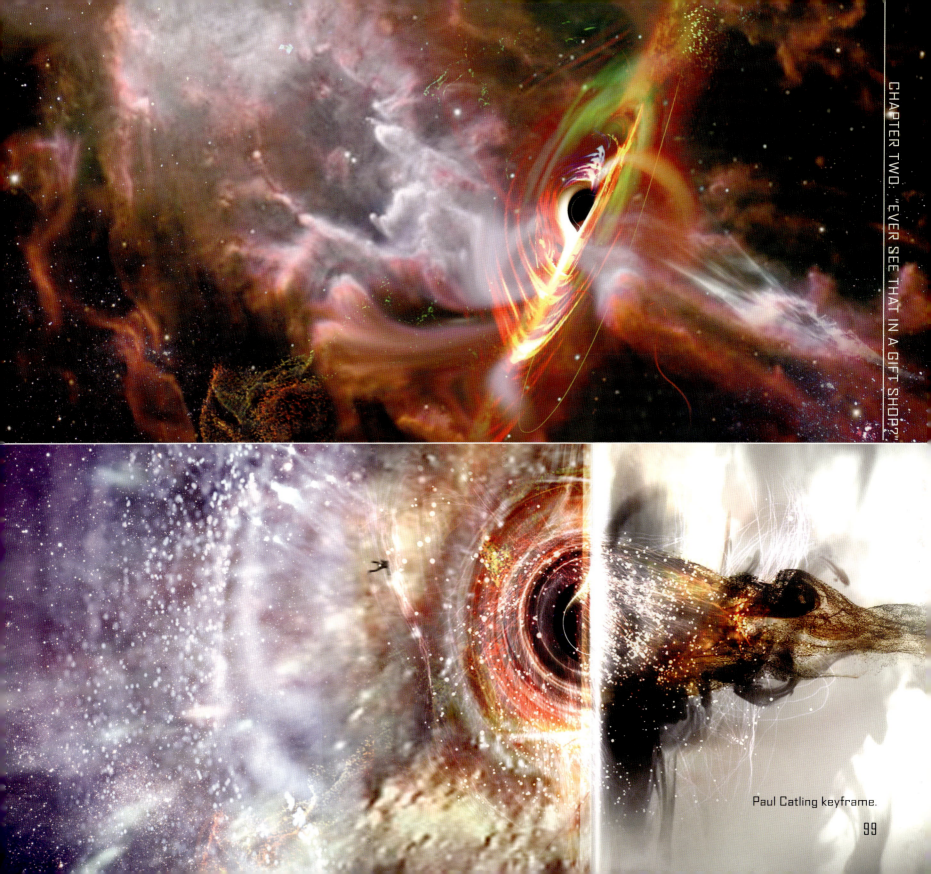

Paul Catling keyframe.

"We always can go back to the comics and look at the great work that Stan [Lee] and Steve [Ditko] did all those years ago," Broussard says. "That work holds up so well, and one of the cool things that they did when they created this character that probably came out of groovy '60s thinking was the idea of magic being from alternate dimensions and accessing the Astral Plane. And the way that we're approaching it is the notion that there's our own dimension—there's the dimension that you and I are in, that we walk around in every day—but certain people have the ability to access a multitude of other dimensions that exist on top of our own dimension, that exist next to our own dimension; that are accessible to us, that are not accessible to us; that are filled with powerful forces, some benevolent, some indifferent, and some not so nice. Some that may want to hurt this dimension. And what Doctor Strange and people like him in this universe can do is access these dimensions, can draw power from them, and essentially that's what creates magic. That's how magic enters into the Marvel Universe."

Roberto Fernández Castro keyframe.

CHAPTER TWO: "EVER SEE THAT IN A GIFT SHOP?"

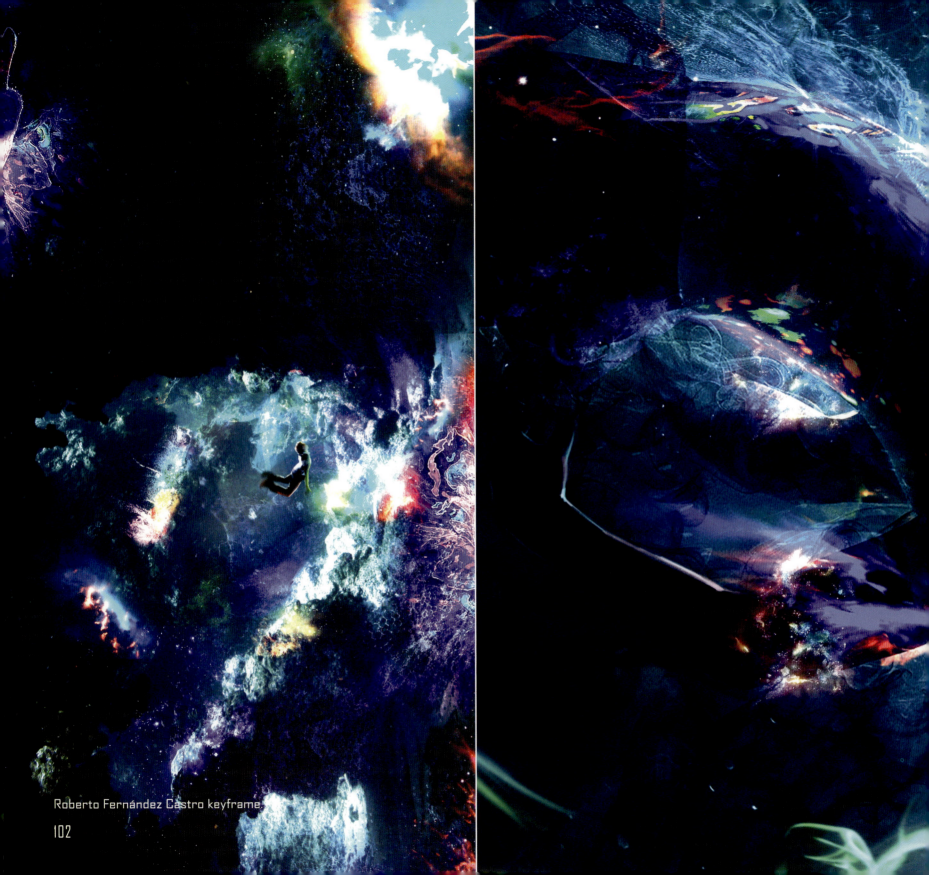
Roberto Fernández Castro keyframe.

CHAPTER TWO "EVER SEE THAT IN A GIFT SHOP?"

Roberto Fernández Castro keyframe.

Roberto Fernández Castro keyframe.

Roberto Fernández Castro keyframe.

CHAPTER TWO: "EVER SEE THAT IN A GIFT SHOP?"

Roberto Fernández Castro keyframe.

107

Roberto Fernández Castro keyframe.

CHAPTER TWO: "EVER SEE THAT IN A GIFT SHOP?"

Roberto Fernández Castro keyframe.

CHAPTER TWO: "EVER SEE THAT IN A GIFT SHOP?"

CHAPTER TWO: "EVER SEE THAT IN A GIFT SHOP?"

Jackson Sze keyframe.

Roberto Fernández Castro keyframe.

Roberto Fernández Castro keyframe.

CHAPTER TWO: "EVER SEE THAT IN A GIFT SHOP?"

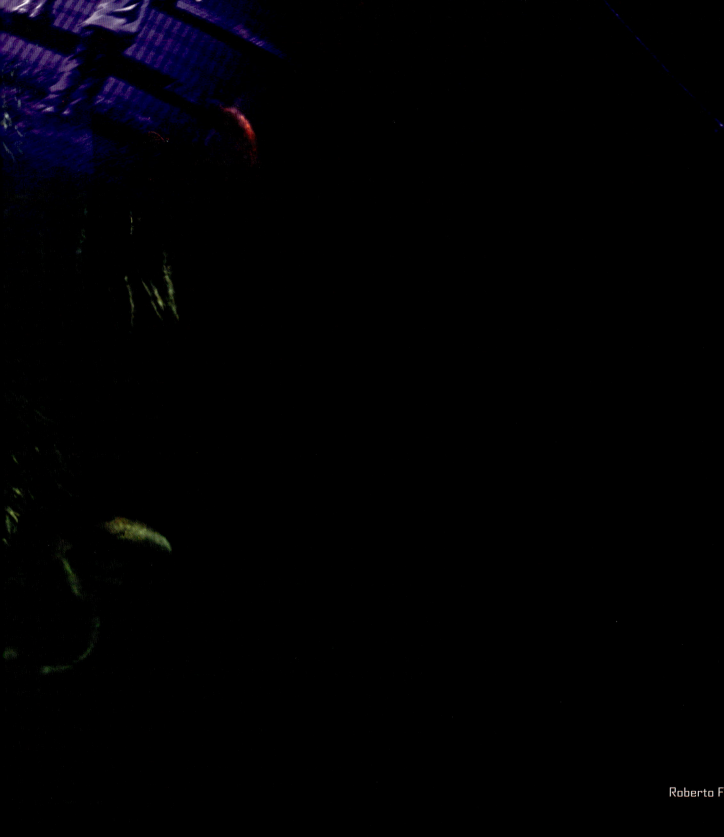

CHAPTER TWO: "EVER SEE THAT IN A GIFT SHOP?"

Roberto Fernández Castro keyframe.

"This sequence is supposed to be very kinetic, very intense," Jackson Sze says. "This image was supposed to be a visual representation of that idea. It's ripping Strange apart—beyond just body and soul—as he travels through an expansive, fantastical space."

Jackson Sze keyframe.

CHAPTER TWO: "EVER SEE THAT IN A GIFT SHOP?"

Roberto Fernández Castro keyframe.

CHAPTER TWO: "EVER SEE THAT IN A GIFT SHOP?"

Roberto Fernández Castro keyframe.

DARK DIMENSION

One of the final stops on Strange's journey is the Dark Dimension, home to one of the most powerful characters in the Marvel Cinematic Universe: Dormammu. "I kept saying, even before the first draft, that the final confrontation with Dormammu needed to be in the Dark Dimension—and we needed to go 'full Ditko,'" Scott Derrickson says. "That was the phrase we kept using. We didn't know how we were going to do it, or what that would mean. We kept referencing the dimensional images in artwork that Steve Ditko did in the early Strange Tales comics—it's so amazing, even by modern standards. It's unique and unsurpassed for what it is.

Pete Thompson keyframe.

CHAPTER TWO: "EVER SEE THAT IN A GIFT SHOP?"

"Specifically, there was a Doctor Strange blacklight poster from 1971—seeing it under an actual blacklight is extraordinary. That became the other benchmark that I gave to Luma, the visual-effects vendor who built the Dark Dimension. I told them I wanted it to feel that crazy, bold, and colorful."

Pete Thompson keyframe.

CHAPTER TWO: "EVER SEE THAT IN A GIFT SHOP?"

Initial concepts, however, saw the Dark Dimension as, well, dark. "It is the Dark Dimension, so we started with a more dark and moody place," Stéphane Ceretti says. "Very green, very yellow, some splashes of purple—colorful, but not necessarily vibrant. In Scott's mind, there was always the idea of 'I like the blacklight poster'—and through all the early work, we didn't necessarily hit that exact mark. So we kept pushing it and kept pushing it and shot what we could, lit what we could, and shot the sequence. When we started to put it together, Scott continued to push and push, saying we needed to go further.

"So, well, we went crazy. We went really, really strong and found a place Scott and the filmmakers liked. It was challenging because when you create an environment, you want it to be photo-real, but you can't have a photo-real environment that's lit with blacklight. It's a different kind of photo-real. Our goal was about capturing the believability with this bold approach. It's potentially polarizing. Some people will find it super trippy and very cool, and others may say, 'What am I looking at?' Regardless, it services the story and the world, the dimensions we've created—which is always the goal."

Pete Thompson keyframe.

Pete Thompson keyframe.

Roberto Fernández Castro keyframe.

CHAPTER TWO: "EVER SEE THAT IN A GIFT SHOP?"

Pete Thompson keyframe.

Pete Thompson keyframe.

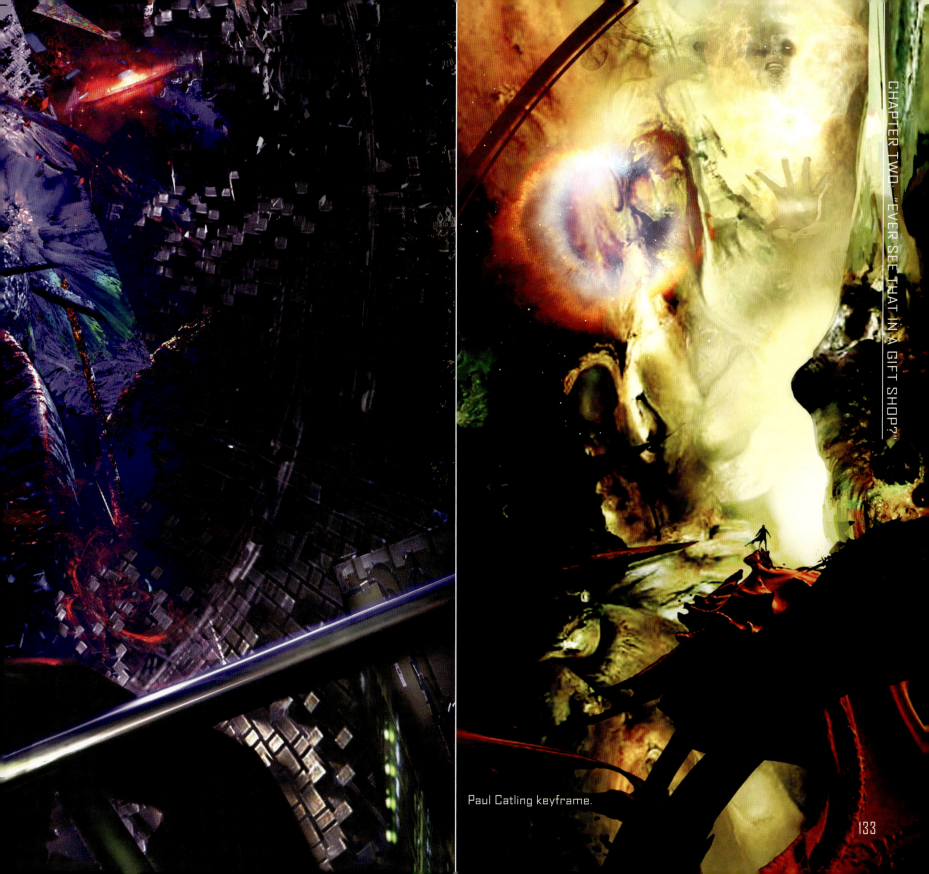

CHAPTER TWO: "EVER SEE THAT IN A GIFT SHOP?"

Paul Catling keyframe.

Jackson Sze keyframe.

The surrealistic journeys through the dimensions required elaborate stunt work. Being tossed to-and-fro on wires wasn't easy for Benedict Cumberbatch, who trained rigorously for the role. "Stephen Broussard and Kevin Feige both said they've never seen an actor be put through more in a film than I have. And also the wire team, the stunt team, are ridiculous. I've done more wirework on this than any other film they've worked on. I've done more than the stunt boys have on this, which I'm very proud of, if I say so myself. You have to be incredibly fit—not just to be bigger, to be someone who would fill the suit so to speak of being this super hero, but also just to have the endurance, to be able to take knocks, to be able to do multiple takes of fight scenes over five days, to do an action sequence at the end of the film where I'm getting flung through a wall one day or suspended by a wire over a drop and then dropped or smashed into an asteroid in another dimension the next."

CHAPTER TWO: "EVER SEE THAT IN A GIFT SHOP?"

Bob Cheshire concept art.

CHAPTER THREE
MASTERING THE MYSTIC ARTS

Despite his initial cynicism, Stephen Strange proves to be a natural in the ways of the mystic arts. His thirst for knowledge and understanding seems insatiable; through his devotion to mastering the craft, we begin to see his arrogance melt away.

"Strange has an edge to his character," Executive Producer Stephen Broussard says. "It's poignant, though, so we really have a chance to watch him evolve throughout the film. That edge begins to chip away, and we start to see a bit more zen. This is a story of redemption, a story about a guy finding his way and learning to be a better person—and in doing so, he really becomes a different person. You look at Tony Stark: He had a redemption, a change of heart. But at the end of the day, he's probably very similar to the guy he was before. He just operates under a better moral code now. He's still a fun guy, still a smart aleck. That's not necessarily the case with Stephen Strange."

"It's an amazing journey to take the audience down, showing a character who moves from skepticism to mysticism," Director Scott Derrickson says. "I think that's interesting—and that's not a slight on skeptics. Because it could be interesting to go the opposite way and to show a character moving from mysticism to skepticism. That's just a range of character development that you don't see in movies. You just don't see it because very few stories really call for it. You see that movement in straight supernatural horror, which I've done, and I'm always interested in characters like that. But here you have something that's not horror. It's a comic-book action-adventure, and you've got a character who's reckoning with what he believes, with what he thinks is the nature of the world, and then being confronted by realities—by very present, undeniable realities that alter the way he thinks about the nature of the world itself. And by doing that, he suddenly has to become much more self-reflective than he has been in the past and re-examine who he is in this world and what his role is going to be. It all gets unraveled for him because of that. I like the idea of a character who's on an intellectual, emotional, and even metaphysical journey."

KAMAR-TAJ LOWER LIBRARY

Bob Cheshire concept art.

In the heart of the Kamar-Taj lies the library, lined with ancient texts revealing secrets of the mystic arts. But knowledge has power: Kaecilius and his zealots steal pages from the Book of Cagliostro—seeking the means to bring down the shield protecting Earth and open a portal to the Dark Dimension, thus allowing entry to the demonic Dormammu.

"As with any interior, it has to look like it belongs to what the audience has seen of the exterior," Concept Artist Bob Cheshire says. "So we continued to reference hundreds of Nepal interior photos that were taken by [Production Designer] Charles Wood and [Supervising Art Director] Ray Chan—in terms of the plaster on the walls, the floors, the color palettes, the carved wood—and then we heightened the design just a little bit so that it was Nepal plus a little bit of something else."

Roberto Fernández Castro concept art.

CHAPTER THREE: MASTERING THE MYSTIC ARTS

Pete Thompson concept art.

WONG

A master of the mystic arts, Wong is the dutiful librarian who also oversees the training yard for new students at the Kamar-Taj. "From the comic books, Wong came across quite like a manservant or sidekick," actor Benedict Wong says. "I think with our version, we're happily putting that to bed and updating his story for a modern audience. Very little is known of Wong at the onset the film, but he slowly unfurls throughout. He is someone who is very serious about his job. He's very otherworldly, wise, and has seen all of that before. It's all about the preparation, getting everybody ready to defend. There's a quiet confidence to Wong. He's stoic. He's forever watching and loyal. I think he comes from a long line of that."

Jack Dudman concept art.

142

Bob Cheshire concept art.

"The library is very old, and the books and artifacts are even older, so the surfaces are more settled and tired, and the colors and materials are more traditional and handcrafted in feel," Bob Cheshire says. "And yet the library is a working space that is used day to day, and so has students on laptops and so on—just like any other modern library.

"The books are special, so we knew we couldn't just put them on a regular bookshelf. They had to feel revered and collected. So Charles Wood wanted these 'honeycomb' rails that pull out of—and go back into—the library walls, which reminded me of curators' drawers full of fragile artifacts in museums, which are part display and part catalogue."

Bob Cheshire concept art.

THE BOOK OF CAGLIOSTRO

Tim Hill concept art.

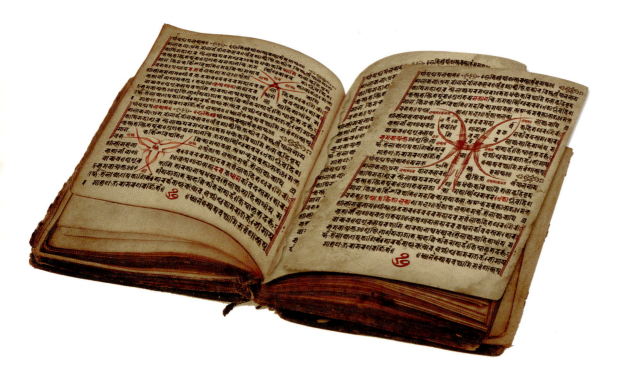

Alan Payne concept art.

CHAPTER THREE: MASTERING THE MYSTIC ARTS

THE EYE OF AGAMOTTO

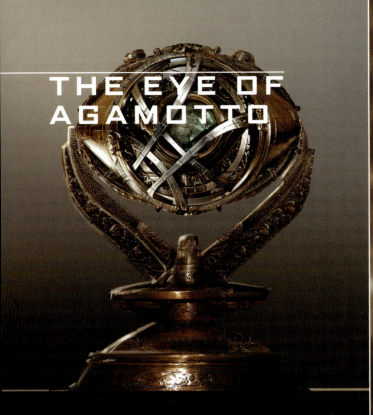

Tim Hill concept art.

Beyond the Cloak of Levitation he earns later in the film, Doctor Strange's iconography radiates from the mythical and all-powerful Eye of Agamotto, an age-old relic with vast magical capabilities. "In the comic books, the Eye of Agamotto has the power to illuminate the truth of any magic happening in front of him," Stephen Broussard says. "So if there was something happening on a dimension that intersects with our own, the Eye of Agamotto could illuminate that and expose the truth of what's actually happening that's hidden from regular humans. It was also oftentimes the deus ex machina—where a situation seems unwinnable, but then, 'Ah! But I've got the Eye of Agamotto!' And suddenly Strange can solve the problem. But it's a fundamental part of his character. So finding a way to adapt that for the story was definitely a priority."

CHAPTER THREE: MASTERING THE MYSTIC ARTS

149

To help recreate the iconic hand gestures Strange uses to conjure magic in the comics, the filmmakers turned to martial artist and dancer Julian Daniels. "In the beginning, they really just wanted to see what would happen if the only tools I had were the script and my own knowledge of the character," says Daniels, who holds a black belt in karate. "I've been a Marvel fan forever, so this is not a new character to me. I knew some of the motions that he had done in the comics. Other than that, I was pretty much working on my own for what I thought I could bring to the character. I think they specifically wanted something that would be unique from any type of magic that's been done in cinema, specifically straying away from vocal spells and anything *Harry Potter*-related or *Star Wars*-ish."

Jackson Sze concept art.

CHAPTER THREE: MASTERING THE MYSTIC ARTS

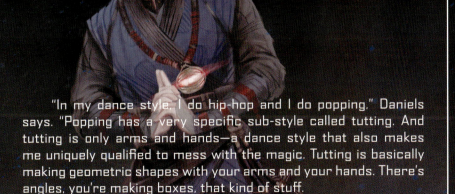

"In my dance style, I do hip-hop and I do popping," Daniels says. "Popping has a very specific sub-style called tutting. And tutting is only arms and hands—a dance style that also makes me uniquely qualified to mess with the magic. Tutting is basically making geometric shapes with your arms and your hands. There's angles, you're making boxes, that kind of stuff.

Then it also breaks down even smaller to finger tutting, where you're doing boxes and shapes with just your fingers. And then it can get really funky where you're just kind of doing alien fingers. But as this stuff evolved, it was more like, 'We want these movements to be bigger. We want them to be more universal, like someone off the street who was coming into this school could learn it maybe a little faster.'"

Karla Ortiz concept art.

TIME MANIPULATION

Concept Artist Jackson Sze created a series of keyframes to illustrate Doctor Strange's early attempts at manipulating time. "The assignment was to showcase Doctor Strange experiencing magic in a low-key setting, in a quieter setting," Sze says. "How do you distill the idea of magic in one scene? This was developed with my supervisor, [Head of Visual Development] Ryan Meinerding. The idea was to depict various places in time in one moment, showing multiple possibilities. Each shard would represent a different possibility, a different time. How do we show time progression affecting a single object? So we came up with the idea of shards—distinct slices of time—that Strange can reach into and select. It began to lay the foundation on how magic could work in the MCU."

Jackson Sze concept art.

CHAPTER THREE: MASTERING THE MYSTIC ARTS

Jackson Sze concept art.

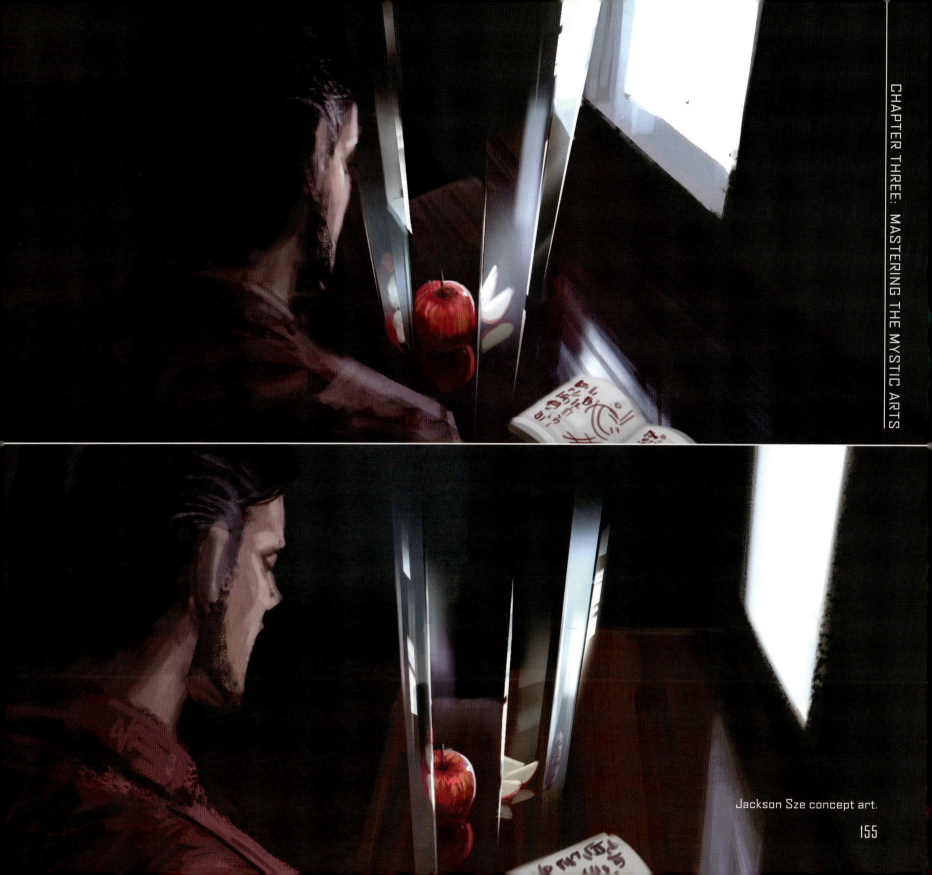

CHAPTER THREE: MASTERING THE MYSTIC ARTS

Jackson Sze concept art.

"One of the challenges we have is that our toolbox for doing new ideas for magic is slightly limited in that we can only do still images," Ryan Meinerding says. "A lot of the things that need to get resolved for a movie of this caliber are really about how those still images get moving. How do we figure a way of conceptualizing and selling ideas about magic that are really only going to work when they're fully realized in perfect animation and perfect motion? So it turned into us doing a lot of keyframe-sequence animations and doing our best in trying to explain how that magic could work."

Jackson Sze concept art.

CHAPTER THREE: MASTERING THE MYSTIC ARTS

"Coupled with the many other challenges, there've been a lot of movies that have done magic, and done it very well," Executive Producer and Head of Physical Production Victoria Alonso says. "We were trying to find that unique element that we're going to bring to the table so that someone could say, 'Oh, I've never seen that before,' or, 'I'm excited to see that'—a version of magic that feels real and plausible, something that allows for the viewer to believe things actually happen. Creating organic elements that magic can give you and not feel overly fantasy, something grounded and mind-bending—the idea that you can do the undoable."

Jackson Sze concept art.

CHAPTER THREE: MASTERING THE MYSTIC ARTS

"The fractal element of these shard prisms created an optical illusion that felt very kaleidoscopic," Visual Effects Supervisor Stéphane Ceretti says. "Scott [Derrickson] really liked that. This led us to what are called Mandelbrot systems—fractal systems. We invented the term 'Mandelbroting' for when the zealots are using the energy from the Dark Dimension—they can transform the world where you see things start to grow and change in fractal patterns. That was another different level of magic that we introduced."

DOCTOR STRANGE'S SHIELD

Strange's repertoire of mystic powers allows him to conjure a protective rune shield made of luminous eldritch light. "Charlie Wood and his team created a number of runes, some of which were based off the comic book, for Strange to use to produce a shield," Ceretti says. "This accentuated the physicality of the magic: He isn't just throwing out a blob of light—he's intricately crafting something with his hands, utilizing these various rune shapes."

Anna Haigh concept art.

EVEREST

Bob Cheshire concept art.

CHAPTER THREE: MASTERING THE MYSTIC ARTS

CHAPTER FOUR
WHAT IS UNSEEN IS ETERNAL

Kaecilius leads his disciples on a quest that actor Mads Mikkelsen describes as "an attempt to make the world more beautiful." A former student of the Kamar-Taj, Kaecilius pledges himself to a higher power for the promise of answers—and power. His zealots, also former Kamar-Taj students, wield a dark form of magic that allows them to split space-time and harness it as a weapon.

Kaecilius and his disciples are marked by a visceral, colorful decay around their eyes. "My character and my followers have evolved a kind of facial expression that goes with his specific cult," Mikkelsen says. "That's a makeup thing that takes about two and a half hours every day. It's like a mask that goes all the way around the nose—a prosthetic mask with a lot of colors in it. Eventually, through added CGI, that mask will be able to open up so you can see through the eyes and see slight, small universes inside our heads."

The major set pieces featuring Kaecilius and his zealots were exhausting endeavors, but Mikkelsen cites Scott Derrickson's approach to the material as a continued source of inspiration. "He definitely takes the challenge of filmmaking seriously," Mikkelsen says. "At the same time he's behaving as the adult who is directing us in the right way, he's also very childish about the whole thing. He loves this film. He loves this universe. And you can simply see his face light up when something is happening, something succeeds the way he wanted to be. For him it's definitely not just a film. It is a mission."

Karla Ortiz concept art.

KAECILIUS

As a former master of the Kamar-Taj, Kaecilius' look mirrors that of the other masters in form and style, save his individualized color: yellow. Head of Visual Development Ryan Meinerding incorporated details highlighting Kaecilius' devotion to Dormammu and the Dark Dimension. "Kaecilius' look developed over time as a result of trying to figure out, first of all, what the Dark Dimension actually was, and then how to represent Dormammu's power taking over. A number of the versions we did were showing how Kaecilius and the zealots slowly became overpowered by the Dark Dimension. We also tried a more simple, cult-like approach by branding them with the symbol of Dormammu on the center of their forehead—the idea being that Dormammu's power could radiate from that."

Ryan Meinerding concept art.

CHAPTER FOUR: WHAT IS UNSEEN IS ETERNAL

"I liked the idea of the look having to do with this rapturous moment of contacting Dormammu—the idea of Kaecilius and the zealots seeing the infinite, and it leaving a mark on them," Director Scott Derrickson says. "They don't understand at the time, but this is a precursor to what's going to happen to their entire body by the end of the film. It was a look I wanted to be cool when it's on screen, and to feel a bit harrowing and menacing, but also not too over the top. We needed to feel the humanity of the characters."

Jack Dudman concept art.

167

Ryan Meinerding concept art.

CHAPTER FOUR: WHAT IS UNSEEN IS ETERNAL

"There was an early idea where the zealots would cry—shedding tears of ecstasy—in a religious fervor that allows them to give themselves over to Dormammu," Meinerding says. "Through those tears, the Dark Dimension starts to come into our world. Essentially, that direction was very visually extreme and ended up being too far. Fortunately, some of the early concepts allowed us to figure out a more subtle way of approaching the final execution."

Ryan Meinerding concept art.

169

Jack Dudman concept art.

Ryan Meinerding concept art.

Anthony Francisco concept art.

Ryan Meinerding concept art.

Jack Dudman concept art.

CHAPTER FOUR: WHAT IS UNSEEN IS ETERNAL

"The Dark Dimension is essentially a blacklight color palette—or ultraviolet color palette—so what if it pulled all of the color from our world? As if the Dark Dimension is sucking the life, the saturation, out of the worlds that it consumes," Meinerding says. "So the idea was that the super bright colors that exist in the Dark Dimension are there because it has devoured so many other worlds. In desaturating Kaecilius, desaturating the zealots, it's showing that the life is leaving them to feed the Dark Dimension. The desaturation pass was also a way of making the more saturated colors of the Dark Dimension seem that much brighter."

Ryan Meinerding concept art.

CHAPTER FOUR: WHAT IS UNSEEN IS ETERNAL

Ryan Lang concept art.

KAECILIUS' TRANSFORMATION

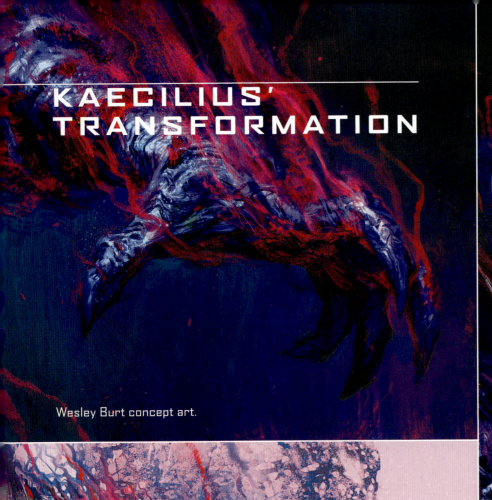

Wesley Burt concept art.

Jerad Marantz concept art.

Wesley Burt concept art.

CHAPTER FOUR: WHAT IS UNSEEN IS ETERNAL

Wesley Burt concept art.

177

KAECILIUS' ZEALOTS

Jack Dudman concept art.

The zealots' backstories evolved as the script developed. In an early draft, they hailed from multiple time periods—including the '20s, '70s, and present day. This gave each zealot a more individualized feel, but failed to convey the cult-like aesthetic the story demanded. Making Kaecilius and his followers former disciples of the Kamar-Taj not only unified them visually, but also demonstrated what happens when students follow the wrong path.

CHAPTER FOUR: WHAT IS UNSEEN IS ETERNAL

Jack Dudman concept art.

The artists took cues from Kaecilius' design to tie the zealots to their leader, also linking the cult to the power of the Dark Dimension and Dormammu. "Using the idea of the Dark Dimension tears, I wanted to explore how the characters' personalities could be influential to the way the markings appeared on their faces," Concept Artist Karla Ortiz says. "What kind of weapon do they use? How do they fight? Are they more mild or more wild? Brash or calculating? This allowed me the opportunity to create distinctive and equally striking patterns that gave each zealot a voice. Eventually, we realized the cracked facial patterns were ultimately too distracting, but they were still interesting to explore."

Karla Ortiz concept art.

Jack Dudman concept art.

CHAPTER FOUR: WHAT IS UNSEEN IS ETERNAL

Jack Dudman concept art.

Kan Muftic concept art.

182

CHAPTER FOUR: WHAT IS UNSEEN IS ETERNAL

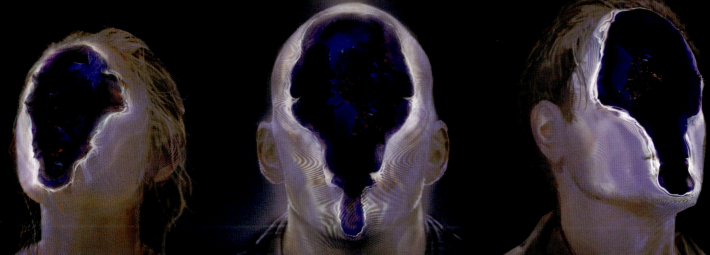

"A word Scott [Derrickson] used numerous times early on to describe the zealots was 'decay,'" Meinerding says. "Trying to find a visual representation of decay, we tried a pass where it was as if they were submerged—like they had crossed a plane of existence into the Dark Dimension—and that the part of them that had touched it had been destroyed or altered in some way. This would leave a very strong, visceral visual mark."

Ryan Meinerding concept art.

Another early concept unified the zealots in black. "I looked at modern cults, exploring the notion that they dressed the same, but something didn't feel quite right," Ortiz says. "You could see this person in the street, though, and it wouldn't be too jarring or out of place. Another key component was, 'What did they look like in their astral form?' There was an early idea that they would become quite monstrous in that form, so I wanted to hint at some of those elements of transformation in the cut lines and overall design themes. Motion was also very interesting to me. Since the zealots had the ability to distort time, how would certain elements of the costume feel moving through time? I added in skirts, veils—things that would potentially behave interestingly when moving in distorted time.

Karla Ortiz concept art.

CHAPTER FOUR: WHAT IS UNSEEN IS ETERNAL

"I actually used my kneaded eraser as reference for how a shape could transform through time, exploring various angles and how they affected the perception of the object. In this specific image, the idea was that as the zealot moves through time, it would create a series of individual selves in different stages of movement—five seconds in the future, five seconds in the past— and we'd see all of them at once. I would shave my eraser down to fit the various forms."

Karla Ortiz concept art.

185

FRACTURED SPACE-TIME SHARDS

As harnessed by the zealots, Ryan Meinerding conceptualized the manipulation of time and space as a dangerous weapon. "All of the sorcerers in the movie fight with some kind of magical weapons," Meinerding says. "The sorcerers from the Kamar-Taj all have versions of Eldritch magic—which is a type of light weapon—as well as casting runic shields or utilizing the magical relics. We were looking for a different approach to the way that the zealots would fight. Since a lot of their power set is about manipulating reality, I suggested that through a series of hand gestures they could fracture space-time and grab that fracture and drag it around, using it as a weapon."

CHAPTER FOUR: WHAT IS UNSEEN IS ETERNAL

Concept Artist Ryan Lang helped Meinerding visualize the intricate notion. "I worked closely with Ryan to explore how exactly the zealots would be able to grab a piece or shard of space-time, and how it would react with the magic Strange was using," Lang says. "It was so beyond any kind of normal weaponry, there wasn't really anywhere I could draw inspirational reference from. All I knew for sure was there needed to be a handle, somewhere, and blades on either end."

Ryan Lang keyframe.

CHAPTER FOUR: WHAT IS UNSEEN IS ETERNAL

Next, Lang needed to determine how such an esoteric weapon would affect its target. "If you're going to cut through something and disrupt space-time, what does that actually do? One idea was that the space-time they were in was drifting in different directions. Or maybe it fractured that specific area they were in and displaced them, causing a ripple, tearing effect. Whatever wound was inflicted needed to feel like it was being subjected to the displacement of time and space." Ultimately, the filmmakers opted for a blend of realism and magic: The weapons function like normal spears, but are created on a whim by fracturing space-time.

Ryan Lang keyframe.

SANCTUM DESTRUCTION

Josh Nizzi concept art.

CHAPTER FOUR: WHAT IS UNSEEN IS ETERNAL

Josh Nizzi concept art.

191

Ryan Lang keyframe.

CHAPTER FOUR: WHAT IS UNSEEN IS ETERNAL

193

ASTRAL ZEALOTS

Like Strange, the zealots can step out of their bodies and into the astral plane. In early drafts, designs for their astral forms focused on the zealots' inhumanity—embodying their fractured existence after they've given themselves over to the Dark Dimension. "There was an idea that the zealots were caught between dimensions," Concept Artist Jerad Marantz says. "So I was trying to design how they were fractured between two spaces. The negative space represents parts of them that were elsewhere—say, the Dark Dimension—while everything that's tangible is currently in front of us. They're in two places at once, sliced in sections, like a series of bands."

Jerad Marantz concept art.

CHAPTER FOUR: WHAT IS UNSEEN IS ETERNAL

Anthony Francisco concept art.

195

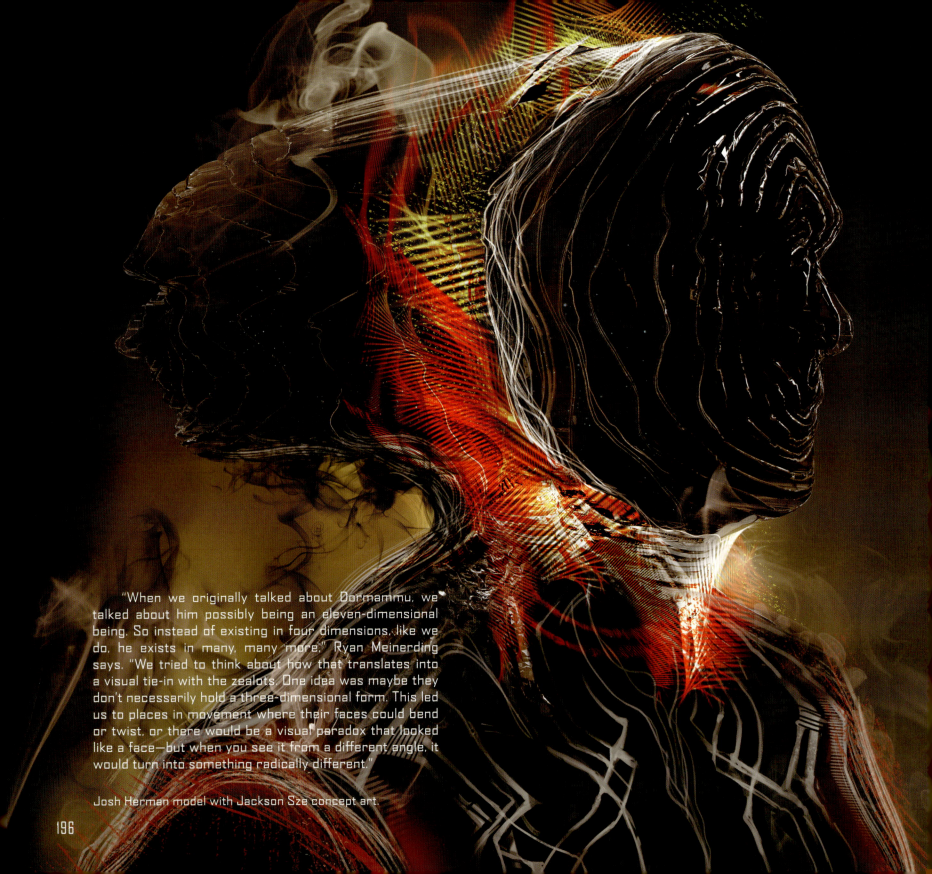

"When we originally talked about Dormammu, we talked about him possibly being an eleven-dimensional being. So instead of existing in four dimensions, like we do, he exists in many, many more," Ryan Meinerding says. "We tried to think about how that translates into a visual tie-in with the zealots. One idea was maybe they don't necessarily hold a three-dimensional form. This led us to places in movement where their faces could bend or twist, or there would be a visual paradox that looked like a face—but when you see it from a different angle, it would turn into something radically different."

Josh Herman model with Jackson Sze concept art.

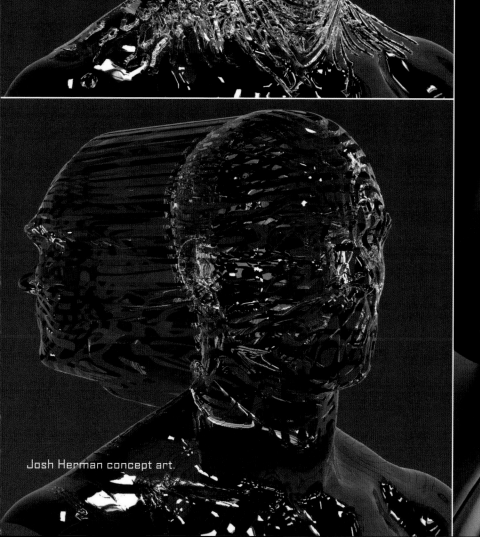

Josh Herman concept art.

CHAPTER FOUR: WHAT IS UNSEEN IS ETERNAL

"We thought about their astral forms being different than their physical forms, but ultimately realized that would be too complicated," Scott Derrickson says. "We were already dealing with such complex realities and dimensions that to give those characters different astral bodies in an alternate dimension was probably going to be confusing. So we decided to keep whatever their normal look was in the real world. Much like Strange, the physical and astral form would be the same."

Jerad Marantz concept art.

"The zealots couldn't be demons; they couldn't be straight-up monsters," Concept Artist Anthony Francisco says. "There was still a shred of humanity somewhere inside them. So as far as we went with some of the designs, we kept it away from overly demon-like or gross. They were twisted, but not in a horrific kind of way. It almost feels scientific."

Anthony Francisco concept art.

Anthony Francisco concept art.

CHAPTER FOUR: WHAT IS UNSEEN IS ETERNAL

"This was an even earlier direction where the zealots were tearing into our reality, and you could see where they were coming from through the path they had taken," Marantz says. "It would only be revealed in their silhouettes and through their trails left behind through their movements."

Jerad Marantz keyframe.

"The biggest challenge on these early passes of zealots was that so much of their design relied on movement, so creating a 2-D image wasn't enough to get the idea across," Marantz says. "Finding ways to get intricate details in negative space, and showing how the design would work at all angles with a number of optical illusions—like having portions of the character missing—required not only an illustration, but also an informative 3-D turntable with almost every design."

Anthony Francisco concept art.

CHAPTER FOUR: WHAT IS UNSEEN IS ETERNAL

Jerad Marantz keyframe.

CHAPTER FOUR: WHAT IS UNSEEN IS ETERNAL

Jerad Marantz keyframe.

Jackson Sze keyframe.

In the 2006 comic book *Doctor Strange: The Oath*, Strange is forced into impromptu surgery after suffering a gunshot wound—while engaging in simultaneous battle on the astral plane. It's exactly the sort of iconic narrative device that defines the character, but recreating the action set piece on film would prove a challenge like none Marvel had explored before. "This keyframe was a way to showcase the tandem events of the astral plane and reality," Concept Artist Jackson Sze says. "If there was a crazy fight happening in the astral plane in a public place, like a hospital, it wouldn't have any real detrimental effect on reality. The humans can't see it. It allowed us to conceptualize large action sequences in normalized places.

"This keyframe was done very early on. We were still figuring out what form the zealots would take—whether they were more on the creature side, or more of a spiritual, almost ghostlike or phantasm kind of visual. I went with a half-and-half, manlike creature with some ghostlike tendrils to represent them."

CHAPTER FIVE
"I TOOK AN OATH"

Sanctums, the sacred strongholds of the mystic arts, together maintain an invisible energy barrier that keeps Earth safe from invading dimensions. If the Sanctums are compromised, the field falls, and Earth becomes a playground for uninvited interdimensional guests. An attack at the Kamar-Taj sends Strange tumbling through a portal into the New York Sanctum—or as it's more commonly known, the Sanctum Sanctorum.

"The Sanctum Sanctorum is a big character in the film, so we had to make it a building with a distinct, individualized personality," Production Designer Charles Wood says. "It's impossibly long. It's never-ending, really. It does weird things. You don't want to get stuck behind a certain door, you know?"

Housed inside the Sanctum Sanctorum are countless artifacts— ancient relics and weapons, including the famed Cloak of Levitation. But before Strange can get the lay of the land, Kaecilius and his zealots invade.

"The Sanctum Sanctorum sequence is a major step forward in Strange's evolution into the Sorcerer Supreme," Executive Producer Louis D'Esposito says. "We see him utilize his new abilities to fight with Kaecilius, and even though he isn't exactly fluid in everything he tries to do, his determination and dexterity keep him on his feet. There's also the beginning of what's sure to be a long-standing relationship between Strange and the Cloak of Levitation."

Strange's fight to keep the Sanctum from falling evolves into an astral-form brawl that spills out into the streets of New York.

Ryan Meinerding concept art.

CHAPTER FIVE: "I TOOK AN OATH"

Pete Thompson concept art.

Pete Thompson concept art

NEW YORK SANCTUM SANCTORUM

"The Sanctum Sanctorum was a location that the comic books did describe, did show us," Production Designer Charles Wood says. "It's such an integral part to the Doctor Strange mythos, and therefore it was one of the first locations Scott [Derrickson] and I talked about. The comic illustrations depict the Santorum as an old New York townhouse—a large three- or four-level New York townhouse somewhere down in Greenwich Village. The address is on Bleecker Street, 177-A Bleecker Street. It's imprinted in my brain."

Concept art by Pete Thompson & Bob Cheshire.

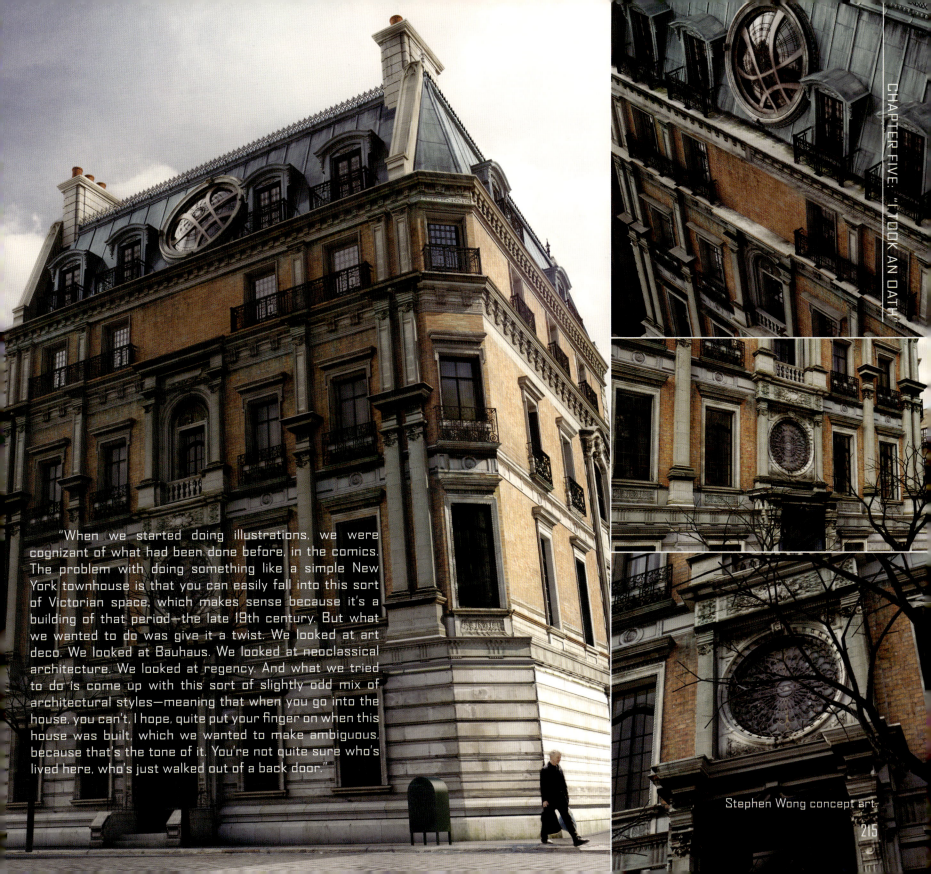

"When we started doing illustrations, we were cognizant of what had been done before, in the comics. The problem with doing something like a simple New York townhouse is that you can easily fall into this sort of Victorian space, which makes sense because it's a building of that period—the late 19th century. But what we wanted to do was give it a twist. We looked at art deco. We looked at Bauhaus. We looked at neoclassical architecture. We looked at regency. And what we tried to do is come up with this sort of slightly odd mix of architectural styles—meaning that when you go into the house, you can't, I hope, quite put your finger on when this house was built, which we wanted to make ambiguous, because that's the tone of it. You're not quite sure who's lived here, who's just walked out of a back door."

CHAPTER FIVE: "I TOOK AN OATH"

Stephen Wong concept art

215

Perception and reality are vastly skewed within the magical structure's walls. "One of the big challenges was scale," Wood says. "How big or small do we make it? I wanted Benedict [Cumberbatch] to walk into the front door and go, 'Whoa...oh my God'—which he did, actually. That's exactly the reaction I hoped he would have, because it needs to be that. It's a Valhalla...The building has its own personality."

Roberto Fernández Castro concept art.

CHAPTER FIVE: "I TOOK AN OATH"

"The color palette was also very influential in crafting the Sanctum's personality. We looked at indigo as one very strong color, and deep, deep blues. Strange is in blue at least for some of the time, so we tried to play on that along with deep vermilions, cochineals, and very deep lacquers. It's very dark, but it's not dark for the sake of being dark. It's just…shadowy. It's mysterious without being creepy—we hope."

More than just a thematic focal point, the New York Sanctum had to serve a more practical function. "It needed to be grand, and it needed to be able to be photographed in such a way that felt epic as an interior set," Director Scott Derrickson says. "It's hard to do. The scale has to accommodate a setting for great action. I knew early on that I wanted Kaecilius and the zealots to attack Strange there—almost immediately after Strange arrives there for the first time. We needed interesting environments for them to interact with, and that's where the idea for the Rotunda room and the Rotunda doors came from, as well as the Chamber of Relics. A room filled with relics behind towering glass sheets became a great environment to have a big battle scene in which we could also introduce the Cloak of Levitation.

Roberto Fernández Castro concept art.

"I think the most important thing is the Sanctum window. The iconic Sanctum window—from both the outside and the inside—plays a lot in the comics and has great power. I wanted the movie to feel exactly that way—that the Sanctum symbol is more memorable than any of the architecture itself. It stands as a symbol for Strange himself, and the association of the symbol becomes tied to his identity."

CHAPTER FIVE: "I TOOK AN OATH"

Roberto Fernández Castro concept art.

"It's fun to take this surgeon who is used to being in the penthouses on Fifth Avenue into Bleecker Street and into a rather derelict-looking brownstone on the outside," Marvel Studios President Kevin Feige says. "Inside, of course, it is somewhat of a nexus between many different realities, and lots of odd things can happen in this building. What's fun is taking a location and making it a character in the film, which Greenwich Village is to a certain extent and which this Sanctum Sanctorum certainly is. Charles Wood is our production designer here and did tremendous stuff in terms of making this film feel different and look different from any of the films that came before it."

Roberto Fernández Castro concept art.

Set Decorator John Bush worked closely with Charles Wood to populate the Sanctum's interior. "We have no idea of the characters who might've inhabited this place as guardians of the Sanctum, or whatever one wants to call them, but you need to put a personality into the place," Bush says. "So you have to try and think through a certain amount of backstory of, you know, maybe somebody had spent time living in this place, studying this place, collecting the artifacts. So where would they have worked? Did they have a desk? Did they have a relaxing area? Had they read magazines and newspapers that they've left around? What were their personal tastes? We don't know any of these characters. But unless you put some of that into the set, it becomes very shallow. Marvel's been very keen that even though obviously there are magical aspects to the film, the Sanctum and the Kamar-Taj were very much based in a sort of historic reality. The place should look used and worn, but at the same time rich and like an interesting, intriguing place to be in."

Roberto Fernández Castro concept art.

Roberto Fernández Castro concept art

CHAPTER FIVE: "I TOOK AN OATH"

Bob Cheshire concept art.

225

"Every set we stepped onto, Charlie Wood just surpassed himself," Benedict Cumberbatch says. "Every single set is a sublime work of art. I mean, the amount of labor, the attention to detail. This stunning space connected to the Chamber of Relics with the very important window back there. And you've got the Oculus. And you've got—if you look around—the finish on the wood, the sort of marquetry on the display cabinets, the objects that have been chosen themselves and how they've been placed, the wallpaper, the tone of the blue and how that reflects the light, the paneling in the roof. Looking at the kind of faux-zinc paneling in this kind of turn-of-the-century, empire—timeless, really—mixture of classical and neoclassical American architecture for this telescopic and slightly TARDIS-esque Greenwich Village Sanctum Sanctorum is utter magic—no pun intended. It is magic. And it's something from nothing. It is extraordinary to work in environments like this, because you don't have to fake it in your head."

Roberto Fernández Castro concept art.

CHAPTER FIVE: "I TOOK AN OATH"

Roberto Fernández Castro concept art.

CHAPTER FIVE: "I TOOK AN OATH"

Concept art by Bob Cheshire & Tim Hill.

CHAMBER OF RELICS

"The Chamber of Relics is at the top of the staircase in the Sanctum," John Bush says. "Here was a place filled with things from other Marvel stories and Marvel characters. We also had cabinets full of pieces which could've been imaginary characters or maybe Marvel stories yet untold. Everything needed to be slightly intriguing and mysterious. But it also needed to be an area—a study within—where you felt that, whomever is the guardian of the Sanctum, that's where they would work and operate from."

Roberto Fernández Castro concept art.

DAGGERS OF DAVEROTH

Tim Hill concept art.

CHAPTER FIVE: "I TOOK AN OATH"

Tim Hill concept art.

EBONY BLADE

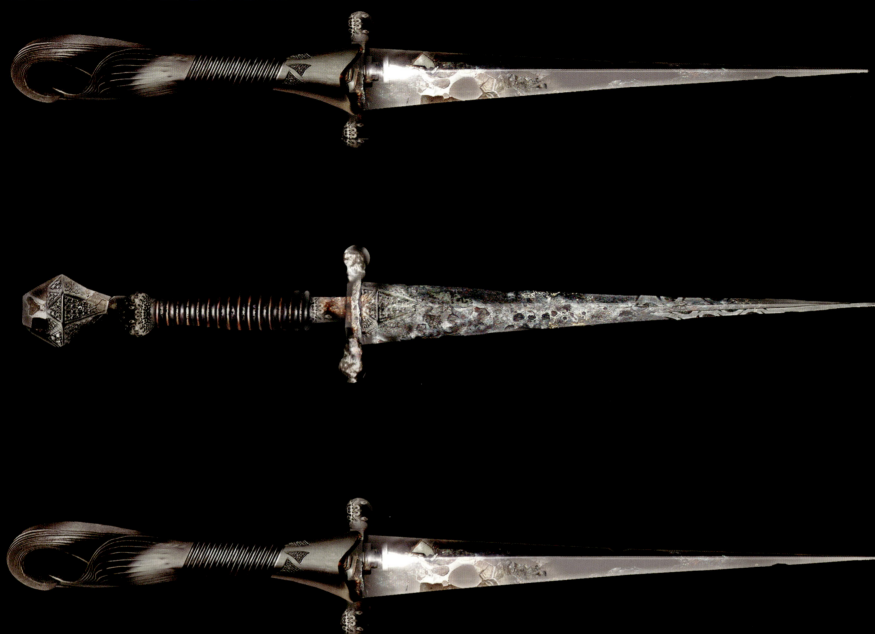

Paul Catling concept art.

CHAPTER FIVE: "I TOOK AN OATH"

Paul Catling concept art.

235

Tim Hill concept art.

QUARTERSTAVES

Tim Hill concept art.

CHAPTER FIVE: "I TOOK AN OATH"

LAMP OF ICTHALON

Tim Hill concept art.

Tim Hill concept art.

Tim Hill concept art.

CHAPTER FIVE: "I TOOK AN OATH"

Jackson Sze concept art.

241

CRIMSON BANDS OF CYTTORAK

Tim Hill concept art.

Tim Hill concept art.

CHAPTER FIVE: "I TOOK AN OATH"

243

Tim Hill concept art.

CHAPTER FIVE: "I TOOK AN OATH"

Tim Hill concept art.

245

THE CLOAK OF LEVITATION

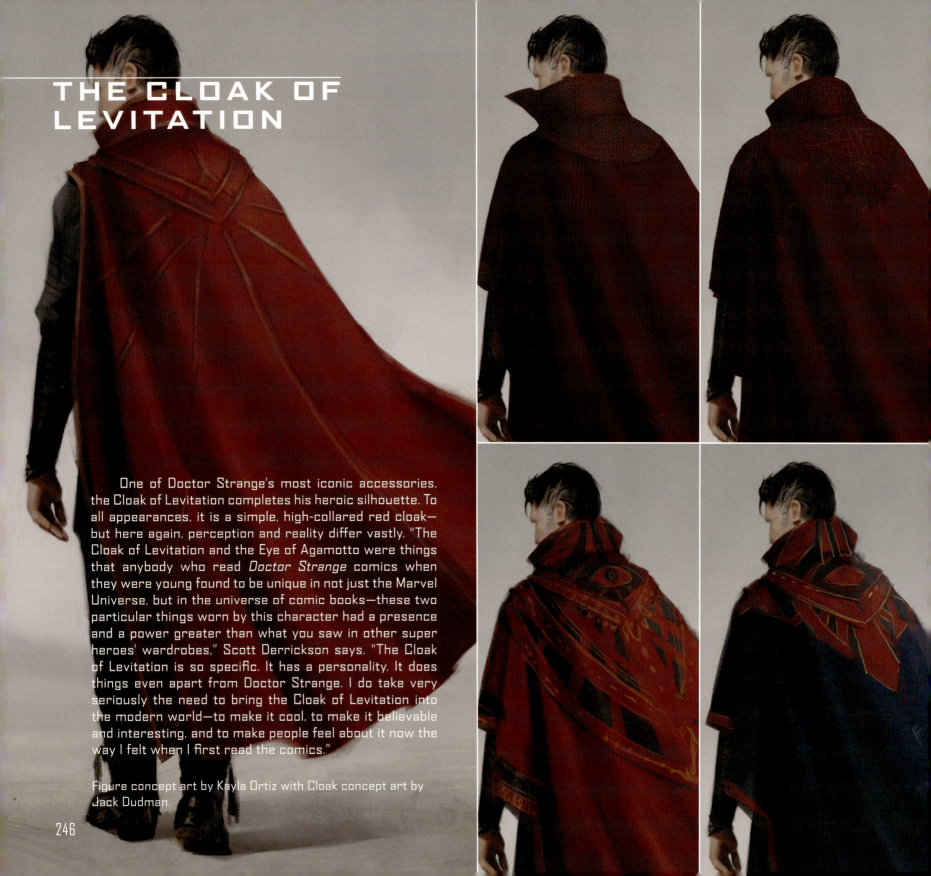

One of Doctor Strange's most iconic accessories, the Cloak of Levitation completes his heroic silhouette. To all appearances, it is a simple, high-collared red cloak—but here again, perception and reality differ vastly. "The Cloak of Levitation and the Eye of Agamotto were things that anybody who read *Doctor Strange* comics when they were young found to be unique in not just the Marvel Universe, but in the universe of comic books—these two particular things worn by this character had a presence and a power greater than what you saw in other super heroes' wardrobes," Scott Derrickson says. "The Cloak of Levitation is so specific. It has a personality. It does things even apart from Doctor Strange. I do take very seriously the need to bring the Cloak of Levitation into the modern world—to make it cool, to make it believable and interesting, and to make people feel about it now the way I felt when I first read the comics."

Figure concept art by Kayla Ortiz with Cloak concept art by Jack Dudman.

"The cloak was a huge challenge because it has to do so many things," Costume Designer Alexandra Byrne says. "It needs to be original. It needs to move. It needs to behave. It needs to be extraordinary. It needs to be unknown. You can draw to a certain point, but after that it is about making prototypes and twirling—because it's all about the weight of the fabric, how the fabric moves, how it drapes. So we just started fabricating, and we ended up with a kind of graveyard of prototypes. It's a lot of red hanging on rails. But that's part of the process. I wanted to really continue the idea of the tone-on-tone detail: There's embroidery. There's leatherwork. There's flocking. There's printing, and many more things. It just adds up to this being, this sentient cloak."

Figure concept art by Kayla Ortiz with Cloak concept art by Jack Dudman.

Concept art by Ryan Meinerding with Karla Ortiz (facial features).

CHAPTER FIVE: "I TOOK AN OATH"

Rodney Fuentebella concept art.

CHAPTER FIVE: "I TOOK AN OATH"

Byrne worked with Concept Artist Rodney Fuentebella and others to study the cloak's movement and shape. "It's got a life of its own—literally," Byrne says. "One of the challenges with the cloak is that it's an asymmetrical design. But I felt that it's very important that it had a symmetrical silhouette. One of the technical things that was very important is that the silhouette of all the characters is going to become huge and important in these different worlds. The hit of color on the screen is going to be enormous when you go into the more psychedelic worlds. So for a moment while you're taking that in, your character is going to become a silhouette, even if they're in full color. But they are still going to read as that until the audience has their bearings within this world."

"The cloak always has a bit of story within the script," Visual Effects Supervisor Stéphane Ceretti says. "But also when the stunt team came in and started to do stunt work, they started to integrate more of the cloak into the fights. They really took it and made it more of a character in the way it fights against Kaecilius and in how it prevents Strange from making mistakes—it was a real journey of discovery and collaboration. As we see the cloak and Strange interact throughout the film, we see a real bond. The cloak is way more in control of Strange in the beginning—but by the end of the film, it's a partnership, for sure."

249

"There are a lot of capes and cloaks in super-hero films," Concept Artist Ryan Lang says. "How do we make this one feel different? How do we highlight the partnership? I did these rough images early on to try and capture the essence of Strange and the cloak in action, and to answer those questions.

I was trying to figure out subtle ways to hint that the cloak has a life of its own in a way—that the manner in which Strange can fight, fly, or levitate with the cloak is much different than what we've seen before. There's a hovering, levitating quality to it—hence the name."

Ryan Lang concept art.

Karla Ortiz concept art.

CHAPTER FIVE: "I TOOK AN OATH"

DOCTOR STRANGE, THE SORCERER SUPREME

Figure concept art by Kayla Ortiz with Cloak concept art by Jack Dudman.

"The comics are very clear," Alexandra Byrne says. "They're very graphic. There's symbols, there's imagery, there's color. I try to absorb all that and then start talking to Scott [Derrickson], to Marvel, to Ryan [Meinerding]. Then I just put together big mood boards of very, very eclectic visual reference. It's a very exciting part of the process, because some of the images to anybody else would have them asking: What does that got to do with Strange?

But there's something that triggers a moment. You then distill them down to mood boards because you can't just have photocopies all over the place—you've got to actually put them together. So through the composition of those boards and by editing the images down to a reasonable amount, you begin—without realizing it—to make decisions.

And then I discuss the boards with Scott and with Benedict [Cumberbatch]. We begin to formulate ideas. I think for me one of the big challenges was obviously in the comic book, Strange has the 'Strange symbol' on his chest. The challenge was how to incorporate that without making him look like 'I'm wearing a graphic T-shirt!' So that was one of the things I wanted to do. And in a way the solution to that influenced the whole look of the Kamar-Taj, because obviously the most important character is Strange. We have to get him right. We have to make him work. And then we sort of retrofitted the look of the Kamar-Taj to support where we'd got his image to."

Kayla Ortiz concept art.

The members of Marvel's Visual Development team are well accustomed to translating complicated comic-book costumes for the screen, but Strange presented new difficulties. "I think Doctor Strange is interesting because he actually has more accessories and more iconic elements of himself than most of the characters we've worked on," Head of Visual Development Ryan Meinerding says. "Between the gray in his hair, the goatee, the high, red collar, the Eye of Agamotto, the symbol on his chest, the blue tunic, the scars on his hands—that's a number of elements, where most times we're dealing with only two or three. It was an interesting challenge. Does the Eye of Agamotto clasp around his neck? Is it tight? Is it loose and hanging? How is the cloak held on? Is there a clasp on that, too? Is the blue strong and saturated enough? Trying to design around all of these distinct and equally important parameters was quite challenging."

Ryan Meinerding concept art.

Ryan Meinerding concept art.

Andy Park concept art.

CHAPTER FIVE: "I TOOK AN OATH"

"We assumed going into the movie that we would have to face that problem of how such an outrageous-looking character in such a bold costume fits into a normal environment," Derrickson says. "It was the same problem that Marvel had to deal with on *Thor*. It just ended up being a problem we didn't have to address, because the story organically became one where he was never really out walking the streets of New York in that costume. So it wasn't really designed to be that way—it wasn't something we were trying to avoid, we just found ourselves one day realizing there isn't any point where normal people ever see him. It might be an issue in future movies, but not in this one."

Ryan Meinerding concept art.

Ryan Meinerding concept art.

"Scott's initial response to that was to come up with a look that feels high-fashion, that looks all right walking down the streets of New York—and then at a moment's notice could become a full-on Doctor Strange costume," Meinerding says. "We did a number of explorations into jackets and coats and fashionable men's outerwear that felt heightened but not traditionally 'super hero'—but could take a few steps to become a super-hero look. I did quite a few animation sequences along those lines. While working on those types of jackets, we were also developing the asymmetrical cloak. I was trying to come up with embroidery that could change and morph into different shapes and therefore be part of the magic of the garment. Alex and I had talked a lot about possibly all of the masters' costumes having been embroidered over hundreds of years—so something like the Cloak of Levitation could have taken hundreds of years to be woven and embroidered. In that amount of time, it had been endowed with its powers. I was looking at a lot of different string art where the patterns feel geometric and mathematical—like they are less decorative and more representative of some higher truth."

Andy Park concept art.

CHAPTER FIVE: "I TOOK AN OATH"

Ryan Meinerding concept art.

"The artwork from Karla, from Ryan, was massively helpful envisaging this character in three dimensions—his physicality and his overall aesthetic, including facial hair," Benedict Cumberbatch says. "He gets more and more complete as the film goes on. He earns every single item of clothing. We wanted to mark that sort of progression very clearly. It's really important—all of that detailing for an actor to help build a character. That was all something from nothing, for both makeup and costume."

Rodney Fuentebella concept art.

CHAPTER FIVE: "I TOOK AN OATH"

"I wanted to have fun with the character," says Concept Artist Karla Ortiz, who designed Strange's final look. "I tried to keep in mind what the vibe would be meeting him face-to-face after his training at the Kamar-Taj. Obviously it was influenced by Eastern culture, but I wanted it to be non-specific. I grabbed elements that were inspiring to me and followed modern couture cuts, particularly in the neckline. I wanted it to feel strong and accentuate his heroism, to convey a heroic silhouette. From the very beginning, I also needed to keep in mind the cloak, designing it all together so it fits together like a puzzle. I wanted certain lines on the cloak to be diagonal or tilted—pointing toward the Eye of Agamotto around his neck. For when the cloak is off, there are a number of small cues and points of interest. It has to function a whole, not just a series of individual parts."

Anthony Francisco concept art.

ASTRAL PROJECTION

On screen, Strange must master the art of astral projection. The Visual Effects team embarked on a similar journey behind the scenes. "We were trying to find something that's different," Stéphane Ceretti says. "So we started with light painting—an initial idea from Scott [Derrickson]—and we tried to go through that path. What we found out was that these characters, like the Ancient One and Strange, have these big scenes together in astral form, where there's tons of dialogue, and you can't have something that's too distracting. You need to listen to what they're saying. It's more about the story than the effect."

Josh Nizzi concept art.

"We spent a long time trying to make ghosts that didn't look like ghosts and are different, more interesting. We went through so many iterations. Then we decided to step back and focus on something more simple. They still have a lot of light interaction around them—they're interacting with the environment in terms of lighting. Kevin [Feige] put it best when he said, 'It's not so much about what they look like—it's what they do when they're in their astral form.' They can go through walls, but they have to anchor themselves when they fight, or else they'll just float through the wall. We played around with the rules and putting those rules into fight sequences so that the characters have to be conscious about the fact that they have to use the environment. Again, it's also so much about performance. We want to see the actor's face, we want to hear their voice—we don't want to be distracted by a Christmas tree in the middle of the frame. We tried to be clever—but in the end, the clever thing to do was to make them simple."

Josh Nizzi concept art.

Concept Artists Ryan Lang and Jerad Marantz collaborated on early iterations of Strange's astral form. "I initially started by looking at sacred geometry and seeing if that could potentially be the base unit of an astral projection," Lang says. "Like DNA, the double helix, sacred geometry would be the basis for your astral projection. Then it moved into wispy types of clouds and an overall ethereal presence where you would just catch hints of who it was. Then it was a lot experimentation with otherworldly fire revealing who the soul of the person, the astral projection of the person, was."

Ryan Lang concept art.

Ryan Lang concept art.

Ryan Lang concept art.

Ryan Lang concept art.

Jerad Marantz concept art.

Ryan Lang concept art.

Ryan Lang concept art.

Jerad Marantz concept art.

Ryan Lang concept art.

"I was looking at the light reference that Scott created and tried to integrate that into Strange's silhouette," Marantz says. "The challenge was to create something that revealed enough of him so that he could still emote and we could still relate to him. It was a big challenge to overcome with all of the potential light lines running through his body. Inevitably, that didn't work. I ended up doing a lot of compositing with 3-D renders. I sculpted a model of Strange and then cut bands through him and then turned those bands into luminous light sources. I then took that and overplayed them on top of a painting I had done of Strange, then really just played with the happy accidents I was getting with the programs."

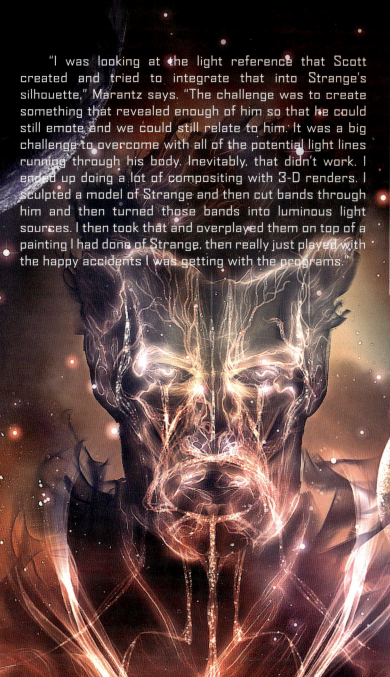

Ryan Lang concept art.

CHAPTER FIVE: "I TOOK AN OATH"

Jackson Sze concept art.

Anthony Francisco concept art.

ROTUNDA OF GATEWAYS

Inside the New York Sanctum is a room with three portals leading to various locations on Earth—including a rainforest, a desert, and an ocean. With the spin of a dial, the gateways shift. Much like the Narthex in the Kamar-Taj, the Rotunda of Gateways serves to spread the sorcerers' influence across the globe. For the filmmakers, the Rotunda was a unique battleground for the spreading zealot brawl within the Sanctum.

Bob Cheshire concept art.

Bob Cheshire concept art.

Jackson Sze concept art.

"Even early on, we knew there was going to be an action sequence in the Sanctum with the zealots," Concept Artist Jackson Sze says. "I was trying to come up with ways that would make the fight interesting. This is not just a regular human, hand-to-hand-combat situation: We are fighting beings with astral powers, with insane magic. And the environment itself is also a huge part—it has its own set of powers. The Rotunda of Gateways was a huge part of the battle, too. While those doorways lead to different parts of the world, I also wanted to relate them to the Sanctum. So when a zealot gets kicked out through one of the portals, you actually see a smoke trail of New York to remind you of where this battle is actually taking place. Super heady stuff."

Jackson Sze concept art.

Rodney Fuentebella concept art.

For the Escher-like action sequence leading up to the Rotunda, Charles Wood and his team constructed several corridors and set pieces that would serve as a base for the Visual Effects department. "We actually built a lot of crazy things," Wood says. "We built one corridor that is on this sort of enormous gimbal rig that could roll. Another one could turn up on itself. We did a lot of in-camera stuff with Benedict himself—no stunt double, which is unusual. We also had to build this enormous set completely in rubber—I mean the entire thing: the doorknob, the floor, the walls, the ceiling, the columns, even furniture. Once you go into these trippy worlds, gravity doesn't behave in the way it should. And these other characters in the film can change reality very quickly. There's a lot of visual effects obviously in all of this stuff. It would be far too complex to do it all practically. But you'd be surprised how much we do in-camera, as well. A lot of people say to me, 'Oh, production design on a Marvel film, what is it you actually do? It must just be a lot of visual effects stuff.' That couldn't be further from the truth. We actually do a lot of the primary effects ourselves."

Bob Cheshire concept art.

CHAPTER FIVE: "I TOOK AN OATH"

Bob Cheshire concept art.

BATTLE FOR THE DIMENSIONS - NEW YORK

Jerad Marantz concept art.

NEW YORK MIRROR REALM CHASE SEQUENCE KEYFRAMES

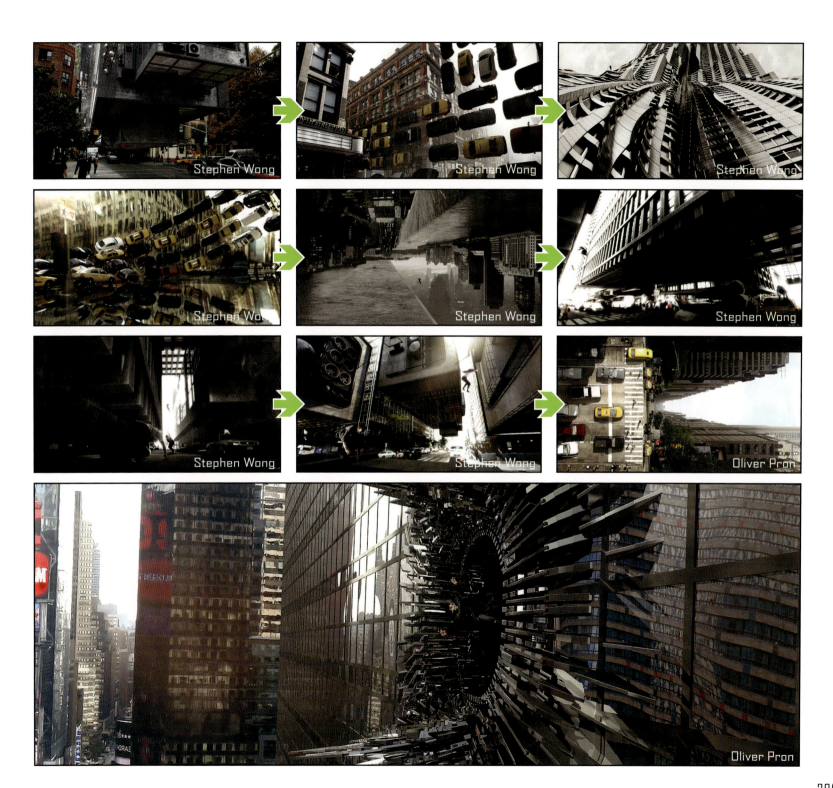

CHAPTER FIVE: "I TOOK AN OATH"

281

Ryan Lang concept art.

CHAPTER FIVE: "I TOOK AN OATH"

Ryan Lang keyframe.

CHAPTER SIX
"IT'S NOT ABOUT ME"

The fall of the Hong Kong and London Sanctums sets off a ticking clock for Strange and Mordo to thwart Kaecilius before he opens a portal to the Dark Dimension—the realm of Dormammu. If Dormammu breaks through, our world will be absorbed into the Dark Dimension, and life as we know it will cease to exist. Even though he's been warned against such tampering, Strange realizes the only way to stop Kaecilius—or at least slow him down—is to reverse time. Strange and Mordo fight Kaecilius and his disciples in real time, while the world around them rebuilds in reverse.

"This is arguably one of the most, if not the most, challenging sequences in the film," Visual Effects Supervisor Stéphane Cerriti says. "It took 20 nights to film. It all came down to planning: How do we shoot this? What order do we shoot this in? We pre-visualized the entire scene and broke it down into stages, but it was still exceedingly complex. We needed to shoot multiple passes of things with motion-controlled cameras at various frame rates—our heroes, background actors, debris, etc."

Before long, Strange finds himself in the Dark Dimension—a realm peppered with abstract inspiration from the pages of comic artist Steve Ditko's original renderings. "Strange versus Dormammu isn't quite what you imagine it might be," Marvel Studios Head of Visual Development Ryan Meinerding says. "Here is this unfathomably discernible being—the ruler of the Dark Dimension, a being who spans multiple dimensions—squaring off against a human. It seems laughable at first, but the execution is actually quite brilliant. It's intrinsically unique to this story and feels completely different than previous finale fights."

HONG KONG SANCTUM SANCTORUM

Pete Thompson concept art.

Pete Thompson concept art.

CHAPTER SIX: "IT'S NOT ABOUT ME"

Pete Thompson concept art.

Pete Thompson concept art.

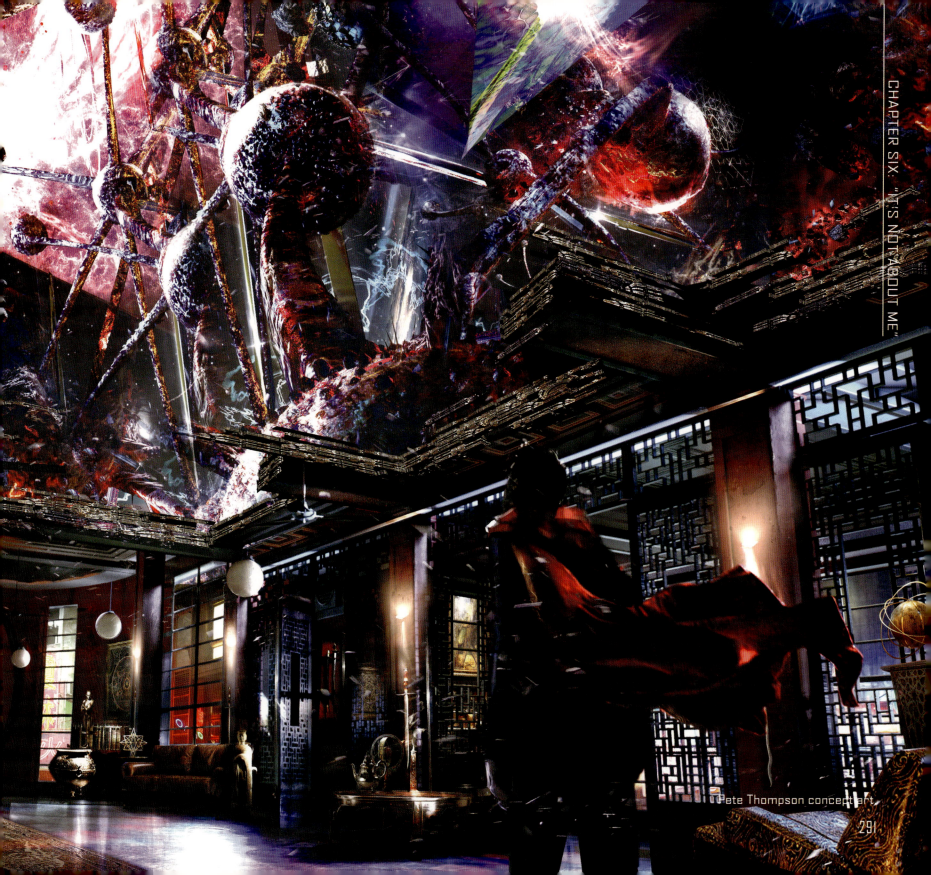

CHAPTER SIX: "IT'S NOT ABOUT ME"

Pete Thompson concept art

291

BATTLE FOR THE DIMENSIONS – HONG KONG

Strange and Mordo arrive in Hong Kong too late: Kaecilius and his zealots are already opening their portal to the Dark Dimension. To save the city, Strange makes the bold decision to use his dangerous ability to manipulate time—setting the stage for one of Marvel Studios' most intense finales to date. "The idea of a big battle scene running forward in time while the world runs in reverse time was really the result of me trying to think about something that would not be possible to do," Director Scott Derrickson says. "I threw it out to the writers and said, 'Let's write the scene, and then we'll figure out how to do it.' It was incredibly complex to shoot. It was worth it, though. It feels like when you're watching it, you're watching a set piece that you straight-up haven't seen before.

"Marvel movies have gotten a reputation for having similar endings where a portal opens, and then there's the destruction of a city. So the idea started by thinking, 'What if a portal opens and the city is un-destroyed, and instead of that portal just being something that gets closed, our main character goes all the way into it, into another dimension?'"

Pete Thompson concept art.

Crew members constructed an entire Hong Kong street outside a UK soundstage. "It's basically based on Kowloon in Hong Kong," Production Designer Charles Wood says. "We went on several scouts to Hong Kong and wandered around and looked at the vernacular of architecture, and looked at how people live and how they exist on a commercial level. This was probably the most complex scene in the film. And what we actually ended up doing was recreating each one of those stores, those businesses out on that street, that exist in Hong Kong.

We matched about, I don't know, 60 or 70 buildings and created this 600-foot set. You want to produce a space that makes you believe you're actually there. We put a lot of time into trying to study and look at how people, particularly in commercial business, do business in Hong Kong: the types of cars people drive, what a postbox looks like, what a traffic light looks like—down to the tiniest little sticker on a handrail, because it's all there. And we need to have it here."

Pete Thompson concept art.

"It's a 360-degree experience," actor Chiwetel Ejiofor says. "You're just a part of it. I love that. Especially with something like this, which requires a tiny bit of a leap of the imagination so often—to have design elements that are completely in control of that, you feel that everybody who is working on the look of the film and the visual landscape of the film is so completely aware of what it is. It really allows for full participation."

Pete Thompson concept art.

"It is one of the biggest, most extraordinary sets I've ever seen, beautifully made in order to be beautifully deconstructed— but in our action, obviously, being reconstructed because it's time going backwards," Benedict Cumberbatch says. "Everyone was talking to me about that set before I stepped on it. And I just made sure I didn't have a little peep before the actual night I first stepped on it. It's probably on footage, my reaction to it. My jaw was scraping on the ground. I could not believe it. It's basically elements of the whole of patches of Kowloon, Hong Kong brought together in one street. It's phenomenal.

"There are presses and metal workshops and restaurants and knick-knack shops and stalls where you basically could cook food. You could go and have something mended in one of those metal workshops. You could have a card printed in the paper shop. They're all functional machines, real storefronts. The only thing that's changed about some of the designs of the neon is we've used LCD because it's just easier to operate in color tone, which even that kind of architecting I think is kind of mind-blowing."

Pete Thompson concept art.

CHAPTER SIX: "IT'S NOT ABOUT ME"

"Every single set is a reminder of how big a film universe you're part of, how big a franchise you're part of. Instead of being debilitating or dwarfing, it's utterly inspiring. You lean into it. You still have to concentrate on your performance being right. You can't scale it up to the drama sometimes of the scenery. But, ah, it's so epic in reality that you sometimes feel that you don't have to do that much to honor it."

297

"We had to constantly think in reverse," Visual Effects Supervisor Stéphane Ceretti says. "All of our simulations we had to do in real time, then in reverse to make sure we got the right amount of motion, and then adjust to make sure we were capturing the right feeling. It's not something you're really used to analyzing in your head. But it's worth it, though—it's such a unique and memorable sequence."

Pete Thompson concept art.

CHAPTER SIX: "IT'S NOT ABOUT ME"

Pete Thompson concept art.

CHAPTER SIX: "IT'S NOT ABOUT ME"

"Industrial Light & Magic came in to add in the top-ups—the digital extensions that go above the set," Ceretti says. "We had to digitally create the Hong Kong Sanctum from a design that Charlie [Wood] gave us, and then we have another big building behind that, which falls into the street and creates all the destruction. ILM went to Hong Kong for a couple of weeks to photograph textures and plates for all the shops and buildings, as well as some helicopter plates. It's a massive digital build because even the practical set pieces had to be digitally recreated, as they're being destroyed—then, with the time shift, being rebuilt. It's a huge undertaking for any vendor, and ILM really did a beautiful job with the sequence."

Jackson Sze concept art.

Pete Thompson concept art.

CHAPTER SIX: "IT'S NOT ABOUT ME"

"Strange and Mordo's dynamic is complicated by the fact that Stephen Strange has great, natural skill and an aptitude for the mystic arts," Ejiofor says. "And Mordo very quickly realizes that he has certain qualities that are engaging and exciting. But he's also reckless and filled with a kind of egotism that maybe is produced by being this great neurosurgeon. What comes with that is this sense of having a certain self-belief, which certainly Mordo reads as arrogance. So their relationship is one of a kind of mentor and a pupil. But sort of typical to Doctor Strange, he won't be a pupil for long, and that very quickly becomes quite important in their dynamic.

Ryan Lang keyframe.

CHAPTER SIX: "IT'S NOT ABOUT ME"

"Mordo has a very unwavering sense of himself—and an unwavering sense of his own ethical, moral universe—which is why somebody like Doctor Strange is such an interesting person for him to interact with. Strange is somebody who oscillates a little bit more, is a tiny bit more flexible—is probably smarter, as well—and thereby is able to use certain kinds of charms and intellects that Mordo is probably shut out of. But they're still very much equals. Their skill sets are very different. They challenge each other in some ways."

Concept Artist Ryan Lang's early illustrations served as inspiration for Mordo and Strange's fighting dynamic. "For most of my keyframes, the direction was, 'Make it awesome,'" Lang says. "Oftentimes, it was about fighting on the sides of buildings, stopping time, going backwards in time while fighting on flying cars—it was about how far you can take this magical realm. I didn't do a lot of quiet pieces. Even before there was a solid script, we had an outline of the abilities Strange had and the abilities the zealots had. I used that to try and capture a composition, a moment, that sums up these abilities—especially ones that are time-based."

Ryan Lang keyframe.

CHAPTER SIX: "IT'S NOT ABOUT ME"

CHAPTER SIX: "IT'S NOT ABOUT ME"

Pete Thompson concept art.

311

The film's dark, chaotic finale represents a departure for Marvel—but one in keeping with the studio's commitment to character-driven narrative, according to Executive Producer Stephen Broussard. "I think when it comes to the tone of Marvel movies, they all should stand on their own, and they should all feel distinct given the different needs of each character and each story," Broussard says. "And that's certainly the case with *Doctor Strange*. This is an opportunity to tell a story that's a little more grown-up and a little spookier—a little scarier because the stakes are real—but of course done in Marvel's fun, action style. I think setting up the world of magic and setting up the stakes of believability that these dimensions exist and that they're dangerous requires a certain seriousness. That doesn't necessarily mean the movie is not any fun. It just means the world is real, these people are dangerous, and this guy has been thrown in the middle of it—and if he doesn't figure out his way through it, there could be grave consequences. Not just for him but for many, many other people. I think that dictates a certain level of grown-up-ness, for lack of a better term, that Scott and Benedict can bring with more of a textured, gothic, spooky feel."

Pete Thompson concept art.

Pete Thompson concept art.

CHAPTER SIX: "IT'S NOT ABOUT ME"

Ryan Lang keyframe.

CHAPTER SIX: "IT'S NOT ABOUT ME"

Concept Artist Alexander Mandradjiev helped design the entrance to the Dark Dimension. "The first thing to establish was scale, and then secondly how we would see it through a lens," Mandradjiev says. "How much could a camera potentially capture and still keep it interesting as an illustration? I wanted to explore the subtleties of the consequences of the portal, the rippling effects, how this could potentially affect what the camera lens is picking up. I wanted it to feel real. I didn't want to create a forced perspective on the portal, so I cut it off in an attempt to create an easier reference for scale.

"He's supposed to be reversing time—so in one image you see a more complete city, while in the other you see the destroyed one. It was done this way so the filmmakers could easily flip between the before and after in an attempt to capture the tone and severity of the pre- and post-destruction setting."

Alexander Mandradjiev keyframe. Alexander Mandradjiev concept art.

"We are dealing with fragmented time, so I wanted to showcase how that affects Strange and his surroundings," Mandradjiev says. "The realm was originally pitched as infinitely vertical, so another issue to resolve was how is he standing on the precipice of the realm—how could we see it going under him? Would he still be standing on a ground plane? It's an optical illusion. There are some details that may seem like a third read or a last read, but they were still important to me. Like the vertical lines running behind him and the fact that his cape bleeds through them: It's like a seismograph of time distortion. It's almost as if, were he to walk through this fragmented time, he would be diced to pieces. I wanted it to feel sharp, like it's dangerous to be in the midst of this time-splitting. He knows how to navigate through it, but there's still an essence of sacrifice for what could happen."

Alexander Mandradjiev concept art.

CHAPTER SIX: "IT'S NOT ABOUT ME"

Alexander Mandradjiev concept art.

CHAPTER SIX: "IT'S NOT ABOUT ME"

Alexander Mandradjiev concept art.

CHAPTER SIX: "IT'S NOT ABOUT ME"

DORMAMMU

In the Dark Dimension, Strange finally comes face to face with the dread Dormammu, a being of unfathomable size and seemingly limitless power. "The idea for the first Doctor Strange movie was that the dimensional power and presence of Dormammu would manifest through the zealots because Dormammu has been shut out," Scott Derrickson says. "He has been banned from our dimensional space by the Ancient One and by ancient sorcerers—an entire legacy of sorcerers who precede Doctor Strange. Now the zealots have broken the grid of protection around our dimensional world, and Dormammu can finally gain access. We save the big reveal for the end of the film when Strange goes to the Dark Dimension to try and attempt to bargain with Dormammu."

Pete Thompson keyframe.

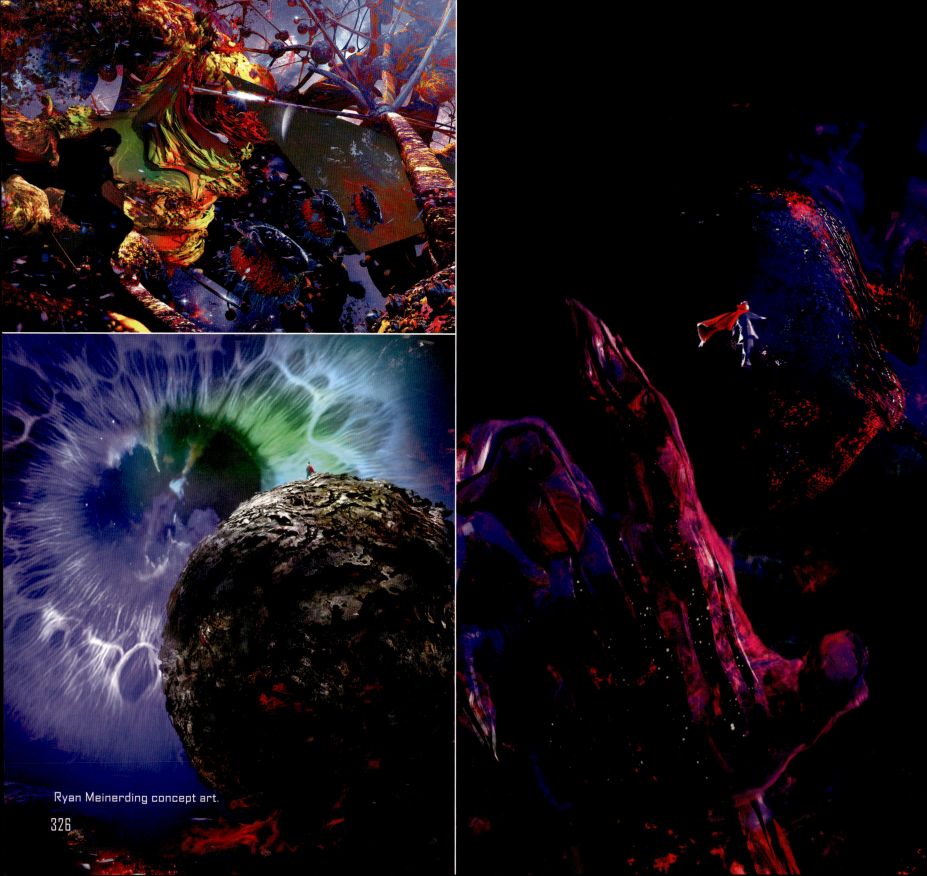

Ryan Meinerding concept art.

CHAPTER SIX: "IT'S NOT ABOUT ME"

Ryan Meinerding concept art.

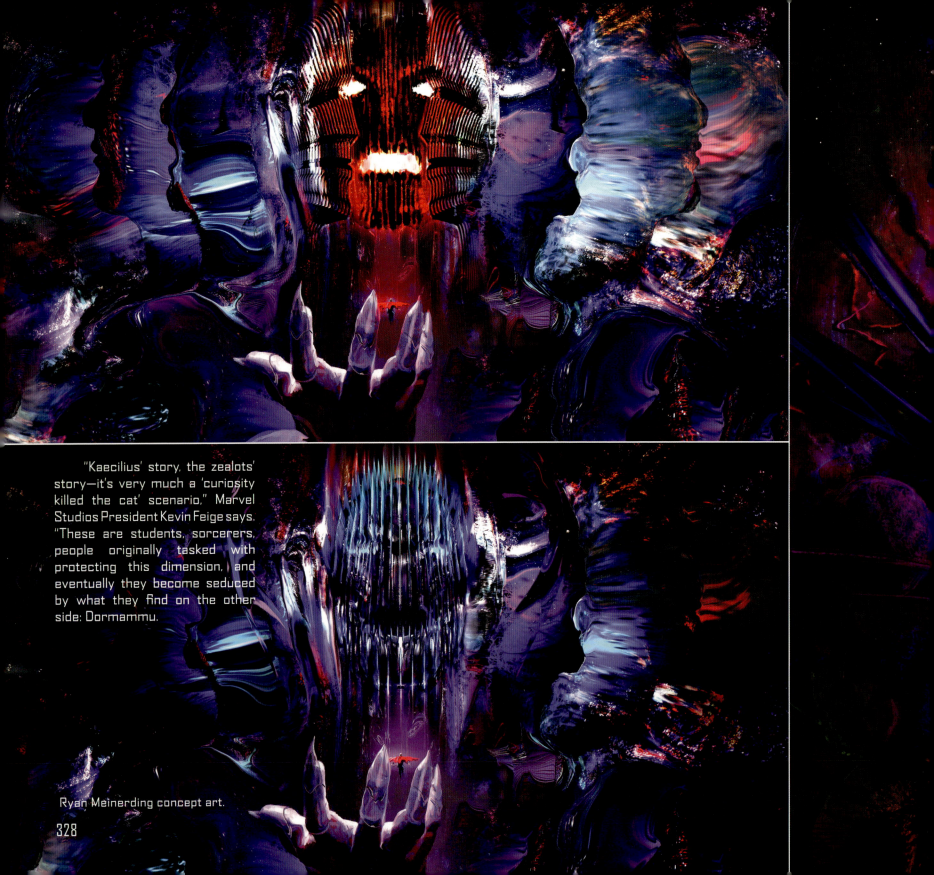

"Kaecilius' story, the zealots' story—it's very much a 'curiosity killed the cat' scenario," Marvel Studios President Kevin Feige says. "These are students, sorcerers, people originally tasked with protecting this dimension, and eventually they become seduced by what they find on the other side: Dormammu.

Ryan Meinerding concept art.

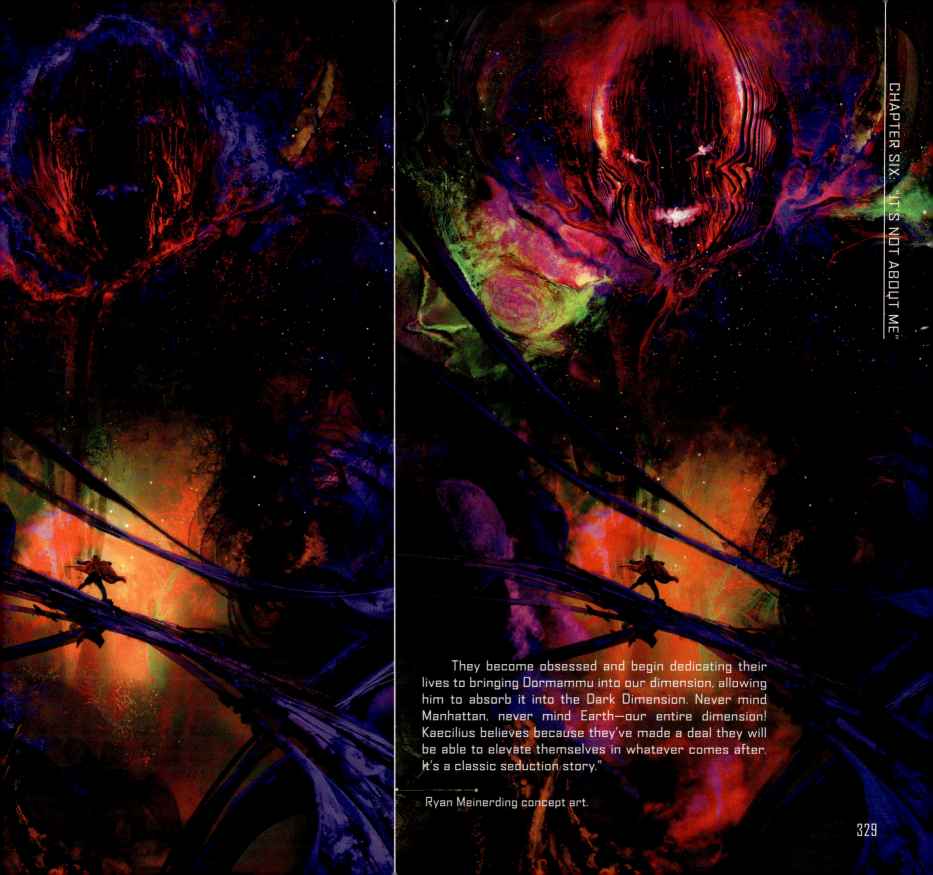

CHAPTER SIX: "IT'S NOT ABOUT ME"

They become obsessed and begin dedicating their lives to bringing Dormammu into our dimension, allowing him to absorb it into the Dark Dimension. Never mind Manhattan, never mind Earth—our entire dimension! Kaecilius believes because they've made a deal they will be able to elevate themselves in whatever comes after. It's a classic seduction story."

Ryan Meinerding concept art.

CHAPTER SEVEN
MARKETING DOCTOR STRANGE

Marketing Marvel's *Doctor Strange* meant capturing the essence of the impossible—and encouraging a new perspective on the Marvel Cinematic Universe. The film's first official reveal came in the pages of *Entertainment Weekly*. The magazine featured an iconically posed Strange in full costume—complete with the Eye of Agamotto—and a glimpse at the visual representation of magic in the film. In preparation, Marvel Studios Head of Visual Development Ryan Meinerding illustrated a series of concepts for Benedict Cumberbatch depicting Strange's more notable movements in the comics. Meinerding also was responsible for the exclusive giveaway poster for San Diego Comic-Con 2016, an updated version of one of Meinerding's earliest pieces for the project.

Alongside the titular character, the visual magic and unique color palette that serve as the film's foundation were chosen as the focus for the theatrical one-sheets. "There's a surreal, dreamlike quality to the film," Benedict Cumberbatch says. "It's a bit more grown-up—and, in a lot of ways, far more internal than some of the other Marvel films. *Strange* is a self-made ship in a sea of reality. Everything is pulleys and ropes, tacking and sails. And yet he's just thrown into an ocean—which as we all know is utterly unpredictable, forever changing, and chaotic." Similarly, the film is an undulating chasm of the unimaginable. "It's an exciting roster of characters, and the earthbound reality offers a nice juxtaposition against the surreality of imaginable worlds that may or may not be around us at all times," Executive Producer Stephen Broussard says.

Early publicity still.

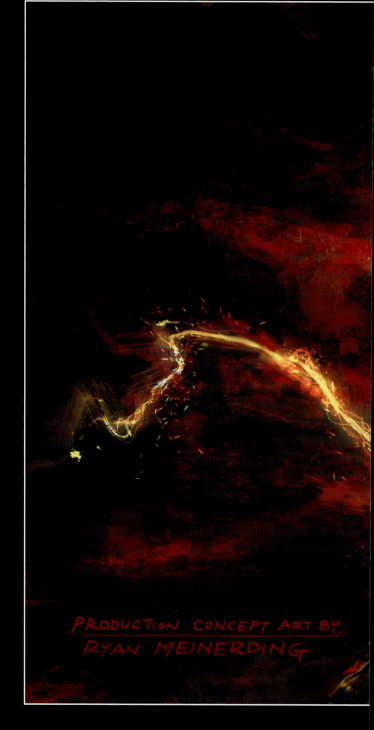

PRODUCTION CONCEPT ART BY
RYAN MEINERDING

Limited-edition collectible poster by Ryan Meinerding, San Diego Comic-Con 2016.

Theatrical teaser posters.

Jack Dudman concept art.

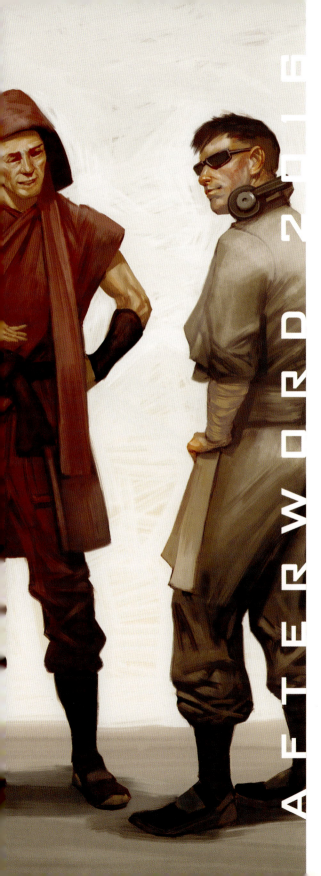

AFTERWORD 2016

The great magic and intrigue of a Marvel project is that no two productions are the same; they each present a new brief and new challenges. But there are experiences that move between projects that are similar, and they form a menu for approaching the solution to clothing a character. This can equally be said about the creative teams. I have been thrilled to be part of the creative process of bringing to life the Marvel Cinematic Universe. I thank Kevin Feige, Louis D'Esposito, Jeremy Latcham, and Stephen Broussard for never humiliating me over my embryonic knowledge of their universe.

There are many steps, detours, and U-turns on the path to delivering a fully dressed, functioning hero, but the starting points are always the images on the comic-book page—the images that first excited the Marvel illustrators and writers, and, in turn, the readers. Then there's the genius of Ryan Meinerding—over five projects, we have developed a close working relationship, allowing us to share our very different skills and knowledge in order to move the characters from a narrative to a defined shared vision. The dialogue we have is the route into taking the costume from the intangible to the tangible and making it a garment that is in our reality, but is also real and true in the world of the story. Jack Dudman and Darrell Warner were key illustrators in the mix, helping me to deliver visuals to define the costume language of this film—with each rendering answering or opening another question as Jack and Darrell draw in parallel with the workroom developing toiles and prototypes. The word "workroom" undersells and demeans the extreme talents that came together at Longcross Studios: cutters, stitchers, embroiderers, leatherworkers, metalworkers, dyers, printers—a brilliant, hardworking team! Add to that the expansive visions of Charlie Wood, Steff Ceretti, and Ben Davis—all of us orchestrated by Scott Derrickson—and anything is possible.

During my time with Marvel, I feel I have surfed an enormous learning curve in the world of capes and cloaks. Thor's cloak evolved from a detour of ideas in the workroom: The sweep of his cloak is deceptively simple, giving him a combination of power and otherness, and was built from a combination of fabrics—one of which is never seen, but would surprise most people in its un-manliness. But undeniably it does its job! The construction method fed into the cloak for Vision in Marvel's, where the piece had to answer a very different brief.

Thor is otherworldly, and Vision is preternatural, and this leads on to the supernatural Doctor Strange. A balance needed to be struck between portraying the magic on screen and maintaining the integrity of our character's clothes, whilst simultaneously counterbalancing the dramatic VFX imagery. The Cloak of Levitation is three things at once: a magical artifact, a familiar to Strange, sentient; a character in its own right; and a piece of clothing. Just as in reading the comic books, where we are drawn in to the characters and the world of magic, I wanted the costumes to draw in the audience—the whole carrying a credibility that allows the eye to rest and discover layers of detail whilst embedded in the world of Strange. Quite a journey!

This book is a testimony to the talent and collaborations that make Marvel unique, taking us toward the world of Doctor Strange.

Alexandra Byrne

Alexandra Byrne

Director Scott Derrickson is behind some of today's most successful horror films—as director, screenwriter, and producer. Known for character-driven films set against an unlikely combination of genres, Derrickson has created a name for himself by making smart films that both challenge and chill audiences. Prior to directing Marvel's *Doctor Strange*, he wrote and directed the 2014 thriller *Deliver Us from Evil*, starring Eric Bana, Edgar Ramirez, and Olivia Munn, and executive produced *Incompresa*, a film by the Italian filmmaker Asia Argento, which garnered excellent reviews in Un Certain Regard at the Cannes Film Festival. Derrickson wrote, directed, and executive produced *Sinister*, which starred Ethan Hawke, from Summit Entertainment and Blumhouse Productions. The film garnered positive critical reviews and earned $87 million at the worldwide box office. Other credits include directing Twentieth Century Fox's *The Day the Earth Stood Still*, starring Keanu Reeves and Jennifer Connelly, which earned over $230 million worldwide; and writing and directing the 2005 hit horror film *The Exorcism of Emily Rose*, which earned more than $140 million at the worldwide box office. *The Exorcism of Emily Rose* won a Saturn Award for Best Horror Film and was listed as one of the "Top 100 Scariest Films Ever Made" by the Chicago Film Critics Association. That same year, Derrickson wrote the drama *Land of Plenty*, which was directed by Wim Wenders and starred Michelle Williams. Born in Denver, Colorado, Derrickson graduated from Biola University with a B.A. in Humanities, a B.A. in Communications, and a minor in Theological Studies. He earned his M.A. in film production from the USC School of Cinematic Arts.

Over the past decade, **Producer and Marvel Studios President Kevin Feige** has played an instrumental role in a string of blockbuster feature films adapted from the pages of Marvel comic books. In his current role, Feige oversees all creative aspects of the company's feature film and home entertainment activities. He is currently producing *Guardians of the Galaxy Vol. 2*. His previous producing credits for Marvel include *Iron Man 3*, which became the second-largest box office debut in Hollywood history behind the critically acclaimed *Marvel's The Avengers*, which Kevin also produced along with *Ant-Man*, *Marvel's Avengers: Age of Ultron*, *Guardians of the Galaxy*, *Captain America: The Winter Soldier*, *Thor: The Dark World*, *Thor*, *Captain America: The First Avenger*, *Iron Man 2*, and *Iron Man*.

Executive Producer and Marvel Studios Co-President Louis D'Esposito served as Executive Producer on the blockbuster hits *Iron Man*, *Iron Man 2*, *Thor*, *Captain America: The First Avenger*, *Marvel's The Avengers*, *Iron Man 3*, *Thor: The Dark World*, *Marvel's Avengers: Age of Ultron*, *Ant-Man*, and most recently *Captain America: Civil War*. He is currently working on *Guardians of the Galaxy Vol. 2*, as well as collaborating with Marvel Studios' President Kevin Feige to build the future Marvel slate. As co-president of the studio and executive producer on all Marvel films, D'Esposito balances running the studio with overseeing each film from its development stage to distribution. Beyond his role as co-president, D'Esposito also directs unique filmed projects for the studio, including his one-shot titled *Agent Carter* starring Hayley Atwell, and the short film titled *Item 47*. The project was released as an added feature on *Marvel's The Avengers* Blu-ray disc. D'Esposito began his tenure at Marvel Studios in 2006. Prior to Marvel, D'Esposito's executive producing credits include the 2006 hit film *The Pursuit of Happyness*, starring Will Smith; *Zathura: A Space Adventure*; and the 2003 hit *S.W.A.T.*, starring Samuel L. Jackson and Colin Farrell.

Executive Producer and Head of Physical Production Victoria Alonso is executive producer for Scott Derrickson's *Doctor Strange* for Marvel Studios, where she serves as executive vice president of Visual Effects and Post-Production. She executive produced James Gunn's *Guardians of the Galaxy*, Joe and Anthony Russo's *Captain America: The Winter Soldier* and *Captain America: Civil War*, Alan Taylor's *Thor: The Dark World*, and Shane Black's *Iron Man 3*, as well as *Marvel's The Avengers* and *Marvel's Avengers: Age of Ultron* for Joss Whedon. She also co-produced Marvel's *Iron Man* and *Iron Man 2* with Director Jon Favreau, Kenneth Branagh's *Thor*, and Joe Johnston's *Captain America: The First Avenger*. Alonso's career began at the nascency of the visual effects industry, when she served as a commercial VFX producer. From there, she VFX-produced numerous feature films, working with such directors as Ridley Scott (*Kingdom of Heaven*), Tim Burton (*Big Fish*), and Andrew Adamson (*Shrek*), to name a few.

Executive Producer Stephen Broussard is Senior Vice President, Production & Development at Marvel Studios, where alongside his colleagues in the feature film division, he is responsible for creative oversight of films on the studio's slate. Since joining Marvel in 2004, Broussard has been involved in many of the studio's film projects. Broussard was an Executive Producer of *Iron Man 3*, starring Robert Downey Jr., Gwyneth Paltrow, Sir Ben Kingsley, and Guy Pearce and directed by Shane Black. *Iron Man 3* is among the highest-grossing movies of all time. He was also co-producer on Marvel Studio's *Captain America: The First Avenger*, starring Chris Evans, Tommy Lee Jones, Hugo Weaving, and Stanley Tucci, and directed by Joe Johnston. Prior to that he was associate producer on *The Incredible Hulk* directed by Louis Leterrier and starring Edward Norton, Liv Tyler, Tim Roth, and William Hurt. He was part of the team that helped usher in a new era of filmmaking at Marvel Studios whereby Marvel began to independently produce films, the first of which was the blockbuster *Iron Man* in 2008. Broussard attended The Florida State University Graduate Film School. While there, he produced a short film (*The Plunge*) that would go on to win AMPAS's Student Academy Award and an Academy of Television Arts & Sciences College Television Award. In 2011, Broussard was named as one of Variety's "Hollywood's New Leaders."

Executive Producer Charles Newirth recently served as executive producer on Marvel's blockbuster *Iron Man 3* and Martin Scorsese's *Hugo*. From 2000 to 2007, he was responsible for the physical production of all 48 of Revolution Studios' motion pictures, including *America's Sweethearts*, *Black Hawk Down*, *xXx*, *Anger Management*, *Daddy Day Care*, *Mona Lisa Smile*, *Hellboy*, *13 Going on 30*, and *Rocky Balboa*. While at Revolution, Newirth also executive produced *The Water Horse: Legend of the Deep*, *Across the Universe*, *Freedomland*, *Peter Pan*, *Maid in Manhattan*, and *The One*. Prior to joining Revolution Studios, Newirth produced 1999's sleeper hit *Galaxy Quest*, along with *Patch Adams*, starring Robin Williams, and *Home Fries*, starring Drew Barrymore. Newirth's additional credits as an executive producer include Brad Silberling's *City of Angels*, Rob Reiner's true-life drama *Ghosts of Mississippi*, with Alec Baldwin, Whoopi Goldberg, and James Woods; *The American President*, also for director Rob Reiner and starring Michael Douglas and Annette Bening; and Jon Turteltaub's *Phenomenon*, starring John Travolta. In addition, Newirth co-produced Robert Zemeckis' Academy Award-winning blockbuster *Forrest Gump* and served as a co-producer on the Barry Levinson films *Toys*, the multiple Oscar-nominated *Bugsy*, and as an associate producer on Levinson's *Avalon*. Raised in Scarsdale, New York, Newirth received a B.A. in Cinema from Ohio State University. He broke into the film industry as a location manager on such films as *Flashdance*, *Pretty in Pink*, and *Ferris Bueller's Day Off*. He later moved up to production manager on *Throw Momma from the Train* and *RoboCop*.

Production Designer Charles Wood began his entertainment-industry career in 1991 as a visual effects art director on such projects as *The Fugitive*, *Under Siege*, Peter Weir's *Fearless*, and Sam Raimi's *Army of Darkness*. Segueing to design work, he has since collaborated on projects ranging from big studio movies to independent films. Wood's other credits include James Gunn's *Guardians of the Galaxy*, *Thor: The Dark World*, Joe Carnahan's *The A-Team*, Michael Apted's *Amazing Grace*, Tony Bill's *Flyboys*, F. Gary Gray's *The Italian Job*, and the films *Wrath of the Titans*, *Fool's Gold*, *Get Carter*, and *Mortal Kombat: Annihilation*. Wood earned an Emmy Award nomination in 2000 for the TV movie *Geppetto* and a 2007 Satellite Award nomination for *Amazing Grace*.

Costume Designer Alexandra Byrne trained as an architect at Bristol University before studying Theatre Design on the Motley Course at the English National Opera under the legendary Margaret Harris. She has worked extensively in television and theater, both as a set and costume designer. Her television credits include Roger Michell's *Persuasion*, for which she received the BAFTA Award for Best Costume Design, and *The Buddha of Suburbia*, for which she received a BAFTA nomination and RTS award. In theater, Byrne received a Tony nomination for Best Set Design for *Some Americans Abroad*, which transferred from the Royal Shakespeare Company to Lincoln Center in New York. Following her work in theater, Byrne designed the costumes for Kenneth Branagh's *Hamlet*, for which she gained her first Oscar nomination. Other credits include *The Phantom of the Opera*, *Sleuth*, and *The Garden of Eden*. She received two further Oscar nominations for her costumes in *Elizabeth: The Golden Age* and *Finding Neverland*. *Elizabeth* finally won her the Oscar. Byrne worked with Kenneth Branagh again on *Thor*, her first production with Marvel, and won the Saturn Award. She then worked with Joss Whedon on *Marvel's The Avengers*. After designing costumes for Warner Brother's *300: Rise of an Empire*, Byrne returned to Marvel for James Gunn's *Guardians of the Galaxy* and Joss Whedon's *Marvel's Avengers: Age of Ultron*. Byrne is married to the actor Simon Shepherd, and they have four children.

Director of Photography Ben Davis' feature film credits include Jonathan Liebesman's *Wrath of the Titans*, John Madden's *The Best Exotic Marigold Hotel* and *The Debt*, Mikael Håfström's *The Rite*, Stephen Frears' *Tamara Drewe*, Gerald McMorrow's *Franklyn*, Sharon Maguire's *Incendiary*, and Peter Webber's *Hannibal Rising*. Davis has collaborated extensively with director Matthew Vaughn on *Layer Cake*, *Stardust*, and *Kick-Ass*. Davis' work can also be seen in the short film, *The Tonto Woman*, which received an Academy Award nomination in 2008 for Best Live Action short film. Davis' recent credits include Martin McDonagh's *Seven Psychopaths*, starring Sam Rockwell, Christopher Walken, Woody Harrelson, and Colin Farrell; Dan Mazer's *I Give It A Year*; Pascal Chaumeil's *A Long Way Down*; and Rowan Joffe's *Before I Go To Sleep*, starring Nicole Kidman and Colin Firth.

Head of Visual Development Ryan Meinerding has only been active as a freelance concept artist and illustrator in the film business since 2005, but his work is already drawing the kind of raves reserved for veterans of the industry. After earning a degree in industrial design from Notre Dame, he transitioned to Hollywood and worked on *Outlander*. Subsequent to *Iron Man*, he worked on *Transformers: Revenge of the Fallen* and illustrated costumes on *Watchmen*. While working on *Iron Man 2*, Meinerding contributed the design for the new Iron Man armor in the comic-book series *Invincible Iron Man*, continuing to cement the strong bonds between Marvel Studios and Marvel Comics. He was part of the *Iron Man* crew nominated for the 2009 Art Directors Guild Excellence in Production Design Award for Fantasy Films; was one of the main concept designers for *Thor*; and served as Visual Development co-supervisor on *Captain America: The First Avenger* and *Marvel's The Avengers*, and head of Visual Development on *Iron Man 3*, *Captain America: The Winter Soldier*, *Marvel's Avengers: Age of Ultron*, and *Captain America: Civil War*.

Property Master Barry Gibbs has worked in film since 1981, when he started his career as a stagehand with model units on *Krull* and *Supergirl*, with the Rank Organisation at Pinewood Studios. He shortly moved to props, where his first jobs included Ridley Scott's *Legend* and the Bond film *A View to a Kill*. Gibbs gained experience in the disciplines of set dressing and standing by on set, then went freelance in 1985 with Julien Temple's *Absolute Beginners*. Three years later, he had the first offer of a prop master position on Roald Dahl's *Danny, the Champion of the World*. At that time, he split his efforts between feature films and commercials. This continued until 1993, when Gibbs went to Ireland for *Circle of Friends* with Production Designer Jim Clay. Since then, he has worked on *Captain Correlli's Mandolin*, *About a Boy*, *Love Actually*, *Timeline*, *The Golden Compass*, *Quantum of Solace*, and *Inception*, among others. Gibbs' avid interest in manufacturing keeps him involved with and running large prop shops with amazing teams of technicians. He was given the opportunity to work for Marvel on *Captain America: The First Avenger*, *Thor: The Dark World*, *Guardians of the Galaxy*, and *Marvel's Avengers: Age of Ultron*.

Visual Effects Supervisor Stéphane Ceretti is a native of France, with a background in physics and the arts. Ceretti started in the VFX industry working as a digital artist for Buf Compagnie in Paris in 1996. He began his career with *Batman and Robin* and then moved to numerous commercials where he acquired all the skills to supervise both shoot and post, before advancing to VFX supervisor for Buf on Tarsem's *The Cell*. From this point, Ceretti has been involved as VFX supervisor on major feature films such as the Wachowskis' *Matrix* sequels, as well as Oliver Stone's *Alexander*. In the last few years, Ceretti sharpened his supervisor skills on various genres of films from *Harry Potter 4* to *Batman Begins* and *Silent Hill*. Ceretti has been overall VFX supervisor for his last two projects at Buf: *The Prestige*, by world-acclaimed Director Christopher Nolan, as well as the latest movie from French Director Mathieu Kassovitz, *Babylon AD*, a Fox/Studio Canal production. He then joined MPC and Method studios in London where he supervised the VFX work on movies such as *Prince of Persia: The Sands of Time*. Ceretti's first adventure with Marvel Studios was to be the 2nd VFX supervisor on the shoot of Joe Johnston's *Captain America: The First Avenger*. After joining Fox Studios to work with John Dykstra as an additional VFX supervisor on Matthew Vaughn's *X-Men: First Class*, he co-supervised with Dan Glass the Visual Effects of the Warner Bros. movie *Cloud Atlas*, directed by Lana and Lilly Wachowski and Tom Tykwer. Following his work on *Thor: The Dark World* as a 2nd Unit Supervisor, he joined Marvel's *Guardians of the Galaxy* as the main VFX supervisor.

Visual Effects Producer Susan Pickett began her career in film as a production assistant in New York, where she worked as a set PA and a 2nd AD on numerous features before transitioning into VFX. She worked as a VFX coordinator on several films involving VFX and animation—including *Fat Albert*, *Garfield: A Tale of Two Kitties*, and *Fantastic Four: Rise of the Silver Surfer*. She then linked up with Marvel's Executive Producer Victoria Alonso, and worked as VFX production manager on *Iron Man*. Now working as a VFX producer, she has been at Marvel for eight years and has worked on *Iron Man 2*, *Marvel's The Avengers* in addition to *Guardians of the Galaxy*. In addition to working on over 30 feature films, Susan is both a member of the Director's Guild of America and the Producer's Guild of America.

Lead Visual Development Concept Illustrator Andy Park studied as an Art and Illustration major at both UCLA and Art Center College of Design. His career began as a comic-book artist fulfilling a childhood dream of illustrating titles such as *Tomb Raider*, *Excalibur*, and *Uncanny X-Men* for Marvel, DC, and Image Comics, among others. After a decade in the comic book industry, he made a career switch and began working as a concept artist in video games and television/film. He was one of the leading artists creating the various worlds and fantastical characters of the award-winning *God of War* franchise for Sony Computer Entertainment of America. Park joined the Visual Development Department at Marvel Studios in 2010 as a visual development concept artist, designing characters and keyframe illustrations for *Marvel's The Avengers*, *Iron Man 3*, *Captain America: The Winter Soldier*, *Thor: The Dark World*, *Guardians of the Galaxy*, *Avengers: Age of Ultron*, *Ant-Man*, *Captain America: Civil War*, and the upcoming *Guardians of the Galaxy Vol. 2* and *Thor: Ragnarok*.

Concept Artist Jackson Sze has worked in advertising, video games, television, and film for studios such as Lucasfilm Animation and Sony Computer Entertainment of America. He is a founding member of the *BATTLEMiLK* series of art books and is a Senior Concept Illustrator at Marvel Studios. His projects include *Marvel's The Avengers*, *Thor: The Dark World*, *Avengers: Age of Ultron*, and *Guardians of the Galaxy*.

Concept Artist Rodney Fuentebella has degrees in design from UCLA and product design from the Art Center College of Design. Born in the Philippines and raised in San Francisco, he has worked on various projects for Electronic Arts, Atari, Rhythm and Hues, DreamWorks Animation, and WIRED magazine, as well as various other entertainment and commercial projects. In film, he worked as a concept artist at Rhythm and Hues before joining the Visual Development team at Marvel Studios. Fuentebella has created key-art illustrations and character designs for various projects including *Captain America: The First Avenger*, *Marvel's The Avengers*, *Iron Man 3*, *Captain America: The Winter Soldier*, *Guardians of the Galaxy*, *Avengers: Age of Ultron*, *Ant-Man*, and upcoming Marvel Studios films.

Concept Artist Josh Nizzi graduated from the University of Illinois with a degree in Graphic Design. He spent the next nine years working in video games as an art director, concept artist, modeler, and animator on games like *Red Faction 1 & 2*, *The Punisher*, *MechAssault 2*, and *Fracture*. Since then, Nizzi has been an illustrator for feature films such as *Transformers 2, 3, & 4*, *The Amazing Spider-Man*, *Iron Man 3*, *Django Unchained*, and *The Wolverine*. He continues to work on video game projects as well as venturing into toys, comics, and television.

Concept Artist Anthony Francisco worked on film and game projects before moving into movie concept art for various effects houses such as Stan Winston Studios, Rick Baker, ADI, Harlow FX and Illusion Industries. Francisco produced art for *Superman Returns*, *A.I. Artificial Intelligence*, *Men in Black 2*, *Spider-Man*, *The Passion of the Christ*, *G.I Joe: Retaliation* and *The Chronicles of Riddick*, among others. From 2004-2006, he worked as a concept artist at NCsoft Santa Monica on the *Guild Wars* and *Tabula Rasa* MMO game titles. Francisco then joined the team at Offset Software as lead concept artist to work on a fantasy-based FPS game. In 2010, he worked at Rhythm and Hues on *The Hunger Games*, *R.I.P.D.*, and *Seventh Son*. Francisco also does illustration work for *Magic: The Gathering* and has been an instructor at Gnomon School for Visual Effects, Art Center College of Design in Pasadena, Concept Design Academy, and CGMW online. He is based in Burbank, where he works on upcoming Marvel titles as part of the Visual Development team at Marvel Studios.

Anthony Francisco concept art.

Anthony Francisco concept art.

ACKNOWL

Victoria Alonso	Paul Catling	Ben Davis	Jack Dudman
Neal Adams	Roberto Fernández Castro	Matt Delmanowski	Kevin Feige
Chris Bachalo	Stéphane Ceretti	Erika Denton	Anthony Francisco
Stephen Broussard	Ray Chan	Scott Derrickson	Rodney Fuentebella
Frank Brunner	Paul Chandler	Louis D'Esposito	Dan Grace
Alexandra Byrne	Bob Cheshire	Steve Ditko	Barry Gibbs

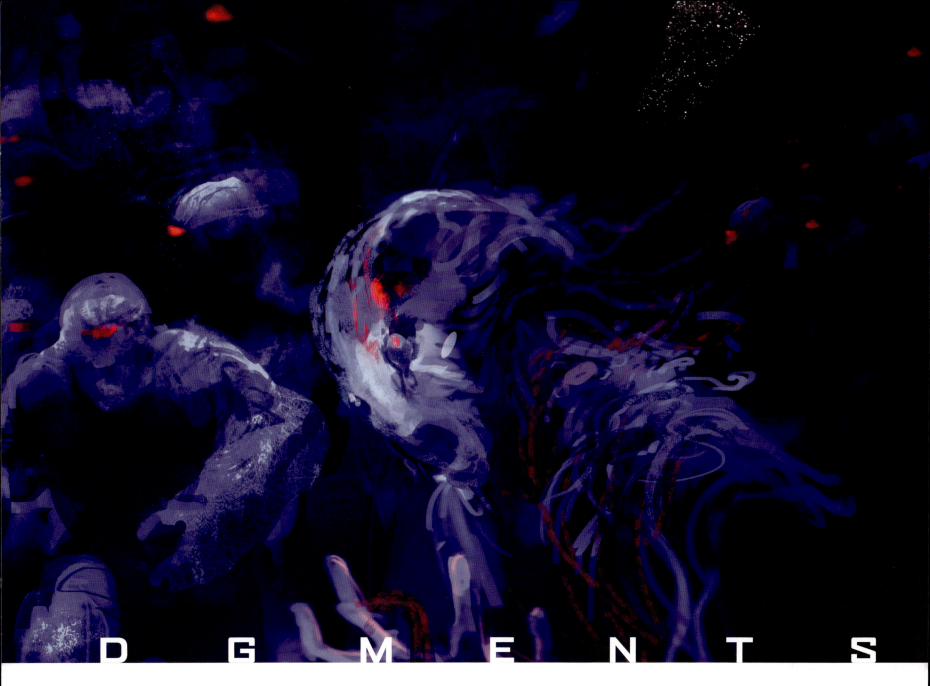

DGMENTS

Tim Hill	Jerad Marantz	Brian Overton	Ryan Potter
Industrial Light & Magic	Marcos Martin	Andy Park	Jackson Sze
Fliss Jaine	Ryan Meinerding	Avia Perez	Pete Thompson
Ryan Lang	Charles Newirth	George Pérez	Stephen Wong
Stan Lee	Josh Nizzi	Susan Pickett	Charles Wood
Alexander Mandradjiev	Karla Ortiz	Jacque Porte	

Karla Ortiz concept art.

ARTIST CREDITS

Ryan Meinerding
Cover
Pages 22-23, 48, 166, 168-169, 171, 174, 183, 208-209, 254-257, 259, 326-329, 333, 335

Anthony Francisco
Pages 2-3, 49-51, 53, 58, 60, 172, 195, 198-199, 201, 261, 268-269, 339-341

Jackson Sze
Pages 4-5, 18-19, 30-31, 74-81, 112-113, 120-121, 134-135, 150, 152-159, 196, 206-207, 241, 266-267, 272-273, 302-303

Ryan Lang
Pages 6-7, 72-73, 172, 175, 186-189, 192-193, 250, 264-265, 282-285, 306-309, 314-315

Steve Ditko
Pages 10-11

Frank Brunner
Page 12

Marcos Martin
Page 13

Pete Thompson
Pages 14-17, 20-21, 28-29, 41, 70-71, 93, 124-133, 140-141, 210-214, 278-279, 286-301, 304-305, 310-313, 324-325

Roberto Fernández Castro
Pages 24-27, 29, 32-40, 68-69, 82-89, 92-98, 100-111, 114-119, 122-123, 130, 139, 216-224, 226-228, 230-231

Tim Hill
Pages 42-43, 146, 148, 229, 232-233, 236-245

Jack Dudman
Pages 44-46, 49, 55-56, 58, 65, 142, 167, 170, 173, 178-179, 181-182, 246-247, 252, 336-337

Kan Muftic
Pages 46-47, 54, 59, 61, 64, 182

Karla Ortiz
Pages 52, 151, 164-165, 180, 184-185, 246-247, 251-253, 342-343

Anna Haigh
Pages 57, 161

Jerad Marantz
Pages 62-63, 176, 194, 197, 200, 202-205, 264-265, 276-277

Bob Cheshire
Pages 66-67, 90-91, 136-138, 143-145, 160, 162-163, 214, 225, 229, 270-271, 274-275

Paul Chandler
Pages 94, 278

Paul Catling
Pages 98-99, 133, 234-235

Alan Payne
Page 147

Wesley Burt
Pages 176-177

Josh Nizzi
Pages 190-192, 262-263

Josh Herman
Pages 196-197

Stephen Wong
Pages 215, 281

Rodney Fuentebella
Pages 248-249, 260, 273

Andy Park
Pages 255, 258

Oliver Pron
Pages 279-281

Alexander Mandradjiev
Pages 316-323

343